PERFECTLY QUEER

Hay House Titles of Related Interest

YOU CAN HEAL YOUR LIFE, the movie,
starring Louise Hay & Friends
(available as an online streaming video)
www.hayhouse.com/louise-movie

THE SHIFT, the movie,
starring Dr. Wayne W. Dyer
(available as an online streaming video)
www.hayhouse.com/the-shift-movie

***

THE ART OF EXTREME SELF-CARE: 12 Practical and Inspiring Ways to Love Yourself More, by Cheryl Richardson

BLACK GIRL IN LOVE (WITH HERSELF): A Guide to Self-Love, Healing, and Creating the Life You Truly Deserve, by Trey Anthony

SETTING BOUNDARIES WILL SET YOU FREE: The Ultimate Guide to Telling the Truth, Creating Connection, and Finding Freedom, by Nancy Levin

THE TOP FIVE REGRETS OF THE DYING: A Life Transformed by the Dearly Departing, by Bronnie Ware

WAKING UP IN PARIS: Overcoming Darkness in the City of Light, by Sonia Choquette

PERFECTLY QUEER

FACING BIG FEARS, LIVING HARD TRUTHS and LOVING MYSELF FULLY OUT OF THE CLOSET

JILLIAN ABBY

HAY HOUSE
Carlsbad, California • New York City
London • Sydney • New Delhi

Published in the United Kingdom by:
Hay House UK Ltd, The Sixth Floor, Watson House,
54 Baker Street, London W1U 7BU
Tel: +44 (0)20 3927 7290; Fax: +44 (0)20 3927 7291; www.hayhouse.co.uk

Published in the United States of America by:
Hay House Inc., PO Box 5100, Carlsbad, CA 92018-5100
Tel: (1) 760 431 7695 or (800) 654 5126
Fax: (1) 760 431 6948 or (800) 650 5115; www.hayhouse.com

Published in Australia by:
Hay House Australia Ltd, 18/36 Ralph St, Alexandria NSW 2015
Tel: (61) 2 9669 4299; Fax: (61) 2 9669 4144; www.hayhouse.com.au

Published in India by:
Hay House Publishers India, Muskaan Complex, Plot No.3, B-2,
Vasant Kunj, New Delhi 110 070
Tel: (91) 11 4176 1620; Fax: (91) 11 4176 1630; www.hayhouse.co.in

Cover design: Kathleen Lynch • *Interior design:* Karim J. García

A catalogue record for this book is available from the British Library.

Tradepaper ISBN: 978-1-78817-875-4
E-book ISBN: 978-1-4019-7075-8
Audiobook ISBN: 978-1-4019-7568-5

Printed and bound in Great Britain by
TJ Books Ltd, Padstow, Cornwall

she doesn't follow
where others go
her life is built
by what she knows
she listens to
the voice within
and wears her truth
on naked skin

and when she steps
into unknown
and starts to feel
the new, alone
like a fish
out of water
the discomfort
it becomes her

and so she takes
it off to see
what lies beneath
the quick unease
painted on
her skin, she reads
the truth she left
for times like these

as fish belong
to the sea
she says
I will always
belong to me

Sara Carr
@iamsaracarr

CONTENTS

STAGE FOUR: THE PEAK OF PAIN

STAGE FIVE: THE SLOW REBUILD

STAGE SIX: FINDING NEW STRENGTH

INTRODUCTION

Sometimes it happens when we're holding hands, our fingers interlaced and thumbs occasionally brushing against the other's soft skin. Sometimes it happens in the middle of the night, when I wake up and turn over to see the roller-coaster silhouette of a body, with its high points and swooping curves. Sometimes it's just when I'm washing dishes in the kitchen, getting lost in my own head, that I'll feel a warm kiss on the back of my neck and suddenly remember to breathe. It's in these moments that I have to remind myself that I am with a woman. Feeling a woman. Holding a woman. This thing that I never thought would come to pass in my entire life is now here and happening. *I did that.*

My brain seems to crave this constant affirmation that she is beside me and that this is real. I'm not sure why. Perhaps it's the number of years that this situation only existed in my mind, and the reality of it is hard to grasp. But my deeper sense is that I'm just in a place that feels completely comfortable and natural to me. With her, it's a place where no labels need to exist. It's just the sense that my soul sees this other soul and feels like it's home—where it's supposed to be. It's a knowing that *this* is what loving fully and with my whole heart feels like.

My conscious mind is what brings these thoughts back to *woman, female, lesbian,* and I think that is where I still struggle to believe, after all this time, that what I am experiencing is real and true. When the memories replay in my head, it's like some dusty old reel-to-reel projector spinning rows of images from the past few decades. From the beginning of the film until now seems like such a Herculean leap that I watch it in awe trying to comprehend how I was the main character that did, and said, and went through all of those things. Where did this courage come from? When was this strong sense of self born?

When my brain starts adding labels to my new life, there is still something that feels uncomfortable about it. Is it because it's new? Is that my own inner, icky feeling about needing to be labeled? Is it residual homophobia from a lifetime of believing that if I became *that* label, I was somehow also becoming a "less than"?

This is why I feel the need to scream from the rooftops that therapy and community are so vitally important in the process of accepting and living one's true identity. The layers of complication and the changes the mind needs to work through are often subtle, but the number of layers makes me think of one of those mille crepe cakes that I have often drooled over but never had the pleasure of shoveling into my mouth. I am resisting all urges in this moment to quote *Shrek* on onions, ogres, and layers, so I won't.

But as I go through life now, I see how I am constantly changing and unearthing new ideas about myself and the world I am raising my children in. I don't want to get stuck. I need these sounding boards, both friends and trained professionals, to add depth and perspective to what I'm feeling. Or maybe it just really comes down to the fact that I need them so I don't feel so alone.

In one of many uncomfortable conversations with a family member who has struggled to accept my new identity, I was told, "The world doesn't need to hear your story. There are plenty of gay people out there now. There's Ellen." It was hard for me to muffle my laugh at the misguided attempt to silence me. Yes. Ellen DeGeneres is part of the LGBTQ+ community. And so is k.d. lang and Melissa Etheridge and Sir Elton John—the list goes on and on. Yet somehow—if you can believe it—I found that their stories didn't feel like being a middle-aged homeschooling mother of two who co-owned a small business with her husband and finally came to the point where she could accept herself as gay. I wondered if Sir Elton ever cruised around in his minivan while wondering how he was going to get the chocolate milk stain from a toddler's tantrum out of the fabric seat.

My coming-out timing happened to be within the same era that Glennon Doyle released her world-famous tome *Untamed*. And, thus, the most common phrase I get after coming out to someone now is, "Oh! Just like Glennon Doyle! Have you read *Untamed*?" I have. Multiple times, in fact. And I adore it. But the tale of Glennon and Abby is still not my story. Nor is Molly Wizenberg's beautifully penned *The Fixed Stars*. Nor is Brit Barron's humorous and touching story in *Worth It*. The reality is there is room for all of these stories to be shared. And there is a need for them. And just as Ellen is out to the world, I am allowed to be as well. And you are too. And she is too. And he is too. And they are too.

But this story is not just for the queer community. In writing this, I became determined to make it a story worth sharing that extended beyond the scope of the LGBTQ+ experience. Because it is. And I wasn't as alone or unique as I liked to convince myself that I was. There was universality to this. Many of us have parts of ourselves that we struggle to love. Many of us hide parts of ourselves or our lives from family or society. Many of us feel unsettled or unsatisfied in midlife and are paralyzed by the fear of change.

I hope that through sharing my story and the many insights that I have spent wild amounts of time fixating on that you can find a common bond. If you've gone through or are going through the process of coming out, this story is my arms outstretched to give you a hug of support and let you know that you're not alone in this and that you're not losing your mind either. If you have a friend or family member who has recently come out, I hope that through my story you are able to have more insight into what they may be feeling and the types of support they may benefit from in their process. If you're a beloved part of our LGBTQ+ community who has been out for years, this is a dedication to you for paving the way for those of us who finally feel free. And if you're my family member—thanks for hearing my whole story.

All I can say is that I am just really, really glad you're here.

IMPORTANT NOTES

This story is told from my memories and recollection of the events and conversations that occurred throughout my life. It's been an interesting and eye-opening deep dive back through experiences that shaped me along the way. Perhaps what shocks me most, though, is the fact that I could even recall so many of these memories in the first place.

You see, I've been teased a lot in my adult life for having a bad memory. Partners and friends laugh in disbelief as I cannot at all recall having certain conversations with them or have no memory of places we've been together. I'm even worse when it comes to remembering the faces and names of people I've met. I once mistook a random guy for my uncle, only to realize mid-ramble that I had misidentified him.

I don't remember these memory issues always being a problem for me. They seemed to creep up more in my life as I got into my later 20s, 30s, and now 40s. My partner kindly reminds me on a regular basis that I am repeating a story to her that I've already shared . . . thrice.

I didn't realize that this phenomenon could be due to inhabiting a body stuck in a stress response for decades, until I read Dr. Nicole LePera's book *How to Do the Work*, specifically her chapter on "Trauma Body." LePera explained that she would go to her "spaceship" to manage her stress, a different mental realm that removed her from present life and current conditions. My friends called mine a "cloud," not knowing that my apparent aloofness was me dissociating rather than being uninterested. LePera notes in her book that with dissociation "some detach so completely that they view the event as a dream. Others develop amnesia."[1] Finally, some answers as to why my brain seemed to delete its cache memory system so often.

You can see the inherent problem this creates in writing a memoir. I share my experience, memories, and recollections through my dissociative lens. Everything in my story is told exactly as I remember it. When I didn't remember how I felt or reacted in a situation, I made sure to say that in the book. This happened most often after I would "come out" to people—regardless of whether their response was positive or negative. I would let my words escape and then immediately retreat to my cloud of safety, barely picking up their response as it washed over me like a passing wave.

My story is my truth. Certain people mentioned in this story have been given a pseudonym to protect and respect their privacy. Nearly all people mentioned in this story have reviewed the chapters (or been invited to review the chapters) to ensure that the key details were correct. With that said, while we can recall the same events, our perspectives of the situation are unique to our own frame of reference. It is not appropriate for me, as a memoirist, to guess what others were thinking or feeling and state it as truth. I can only offer my own perspective and feelings to you.

And now a word about terminology. . . .

Throughout my story, you'll see that I refer to myself interchangeably as *gay*, *lesbian*, *queer*, and *LGBTQ+*. There are a few reasons. One, I am proud of all the titles and, at the same time, not tightly bound to any single one specifically. I use them sometimes for ease or sentence flow; and other times that is the label that feels most appropriate in that moment. One is no better or worse or more right than another. They all have a purpose. Two, the more I say them, the more comfortable I become with them. I couldn't say so many of these words for so long. *Lesbian* took me the longest to be able to utter comfortably. I am undoing a lifetime of conditioning to be at peace with all the labels.

Some of the labels may sting for you. Some may not feel good or right to you. There are women who don't like the patriarchal feel of *gay* used as a broad term for same-sex attraction. There are people who have been out for decades who bristle at the term *queer* for the negative history it carries, whereas the younger generations seem to embrace the reclamation of the word and the fact that it is a blanket term that can encompass both sexuality and gender. As for the acronym LGBTQIA2S+, I have shortened it to LGBTQ+ for the sole fact that if this ever turns into an audiobook, I am 100 percent guaranteed to tie my tongue in knots and inadvertently spit on the microphone trying to get all the letters out.

To paraphrase the incomparable Maya Angelou, we do our best until we know better, and then we can do better. I am a work in progress. We all are. That is the beauty of our ever-changing human experience.

STAGE ONE

EXPECTATIONS

STAR BABY

Star Baby.

That's what my mom called me as a young kid. My mom said something was different about me. She had an inner knowing that told her I was meant for something great in life. We talked about getting STARBABY put on a vanity plate for my first car when I was older.

What would I be famous for? She had no idea, nor did I. It was just mother's intuition that my life wouldn't follow the conventional path. I was meant to do important things. Big things. I hoped it had to do with dancing ballet or joining the cast of *Boy Meets World* and becoming Topanga's earthy best friend who always carried around a sack of trail mix. That would have been the pinnacle of stardom for me.

Instead, things seemed to progress along the ballet route. I started dancing ballet at age four and snagged a role in the Empire State Ballet's production of *The Nutcracker* when I was in third grade. I remember returning to my elementary school gym class after a show, my Victorian-curl ringlets from my mom's pink foam rollers bobbing up and down on my head like corks in the water. My stage makeup had that '80s flair of obnoxious pinks and purples. A boy in my class looked at my exaggerated hair and makeup from the performance and said, "You're weird." I knew other kids in the class were staring at me too.

And I loved it. I soaked up the attention like my brother soaked up Hi-C Ecto Cooler juice boxes. *I am different? Thank you for noticing!* I thought.

The following year, I landed a spot in the Joffrey Ballet's production of *Romeo and Juliet*. It was my first paid job and I made $15 per show, practically a millionaire by 1980s and fourth-grade standards. I remember holding that check for $45 in my hand and thinking, *This is it! I've made it.* I loved that feeling of success. It was like pouring gasoline on a fire inside of me. The rush. The endorphins. I became high on achievement and craved my next fix. I was an elementary school success junkie.

That's also the first time I remember an underlying fear creeping in. The high of achievement eventually wore off, and I would be stuck with the desperate feeling of, *Is this it? How could I possibly do more?* I would nearly extinguish my own fire with the hollow fear that I could never possibly achieve anything greater than what I just had. I wondered if my life had peaked at 10 years old.

I look back on this time and am curious when exactly the seed of perfectionism was planted. I questioned if it had always been a part of me, etched into my DNA through a long line of ancestral perfectionists who placed irrational expectations on themselves; though I couldn't recall seeing those behaviors in my mother, grandmother Jean, or great-grandmother Violet. I wondered if maybe my perfectionism grew instead from my environment, molded by subtle cues from my mom in an effort to make my life better than hers. She was a young mom. She had given up her college career to get married and have me. She worked long hours as a waitress to make ends meet. As a parent now, I understand that we all want an easier road for our children to follow. What was it about the way I was raised that pushed me to a more extreme standard though, where doing well wasn't good enough? I had to be the best. All. The. Time.

Memories of not achieving Star Baby status used to cast dark shadows in my mind. I remember as far back as Lutheran preschool, when I was cast in the nativity play as Random Angel #4. I was pissed, though it's doubtful that anyone sensed those feelings radiating from my chubby pink cheeks and wispy blond hair. I stared at the lead angel as she got to speak a sentence to the audience of adoring parents. I wondered why that role hadn't been entrusted to me. But being lead angel was a lesser worry. I remember my true fixation was why I didn't get to play Mary or Joseph, or replace the plastic baby doll that was Jesus. Why was I resigned to the background, just standing there in my white pillowcase with my cardboard wings, watching others demonstrate their acting chops? All eyes were on them. I could have picked my nose and nobody would have noticed.

My feelings of perfectionism seemed to grow each time I achieved something new. Each taste of achievement only made me crave it that much more. And not being the best, to me, felt like starvation. If I tried gymnastics, I stared at the girl my age who was training for the competitive team and would think to myself, *Why am I not her?* I would beat myself up for having started the sport too late, wishing I could have found my passion for tumbling when I was 3 instead of when I was 11. It was always an internal struggle between pushing myself to work extra hard to catch up to her level, or giving up and accepting defeat because there was no way I would reach the level of success that others had already achieved. I couldn't just be. I couldn't just do. For me it was "be the best or don't be at all."

Perfectionism came out in various ways as I got older. Most of the time it arose as obsessive thoughts after I'd made a mistake. I felt physically ill in my seventh-grade math class when I realized that I had forgotten to do one math problem on my homework assignment. I had to excuse myself to go to the bathroom and hide while the teacher went over the homework problems with the class. God forbid I be present and the teacher have an opportunity to call on me for that one question where I didn't have an answer prepared.

Hiding also turned into lying on occasion. When I couldn't hide my mistakes, I would try to talk myself out of them by denying they ever happened or playing dumb like I didn't know what had gone wrong. By this point, I had learned that I could do all things in life, except admit that I was wrong.

My perfectionism gave me an impressive résumé as a child. However, it also damaged my relationships, particularly with my brother, Steve. We developed an unspoken competitiveness to be the better child and garner Mom's attention. It was competing with Steve that made me fixate the most, and one standardized test consumed me for over a decade.

This particular standardized test was required in second or third grade. I took it and got an above-average score. I liked seeing the black bars stretch across the page showing my percentage of correctness in each category. I was so correct. The bars were nearly to the margin of the page. Steve was one year behind me in school. When it was his turn to take the test, his scores qualified him for a special gifted and talented program.

You've probably heard the phrase "comparison is the thief of joy." It's true. Suddenly, compared to Steve, my excellent scores were now garbage. It didn't matter that one year prior I was content with my work. Now knowing that there was the prize of acceptance into a gifted and talented program burned me up inside. How could I have missed out on that? What was wrong with me?

Every so often I would pull out our test score sheets, printed on a dot matrix printer. I would compare our scores line by line, trying to make sense of my own shortcomings. What made matters worse for me was that I outscored him on nearly every subject and I still wasn't good enough. My scores were higher and yet I wasn't good enough. Questioning turned to disappointment. Disappointment turned to shame. Shame turned to obsession. The papers continued to yellow over the years, and I continued to compare the scores every time I would come across them in a drawer of school memorabilia. Every time, I hoped for some insight that would signal to me that I was okay, that I had done everything right and it was someone else's mistake that I was overlooked. My perfectionism loved blame.

By my teen years it shouldn't have mattered to me anymore. I had achieved other things to soothe my perfectionist soul. By seventh grade I was the first person in my class to earn a varsity letter. My letter jacket hung loosely over my tiny prepubescent frame as I strutted around the middle school campus wearing an honor typically reserved for the burly high school jocks. By the end of middle school,

I won nearly every school award possible, from English to technology to art, in my eighth-grade awards ceremony. I remember at the awards ceremony proudly walking up to the front of the banquet hall to collect another award and having a friend of mine threaten as I passed, "If you walk up here one more time, I'm going to trip you." (She may have been a bit of a perfectionist too.)

By ninth grade, I had been selected as the youngest Rotary Youth Exchange student that my local club had ever sent abroad. I was elated that they chose me to represent our area for a yearlong exchange program in Bolivia. I knew my mom was proud too, even if she was equally terrified to send her young child overseas in a pre-Internet era.

That year abroad held me back academically. When I returned to the U.S., my class credits from Bolivia didn't count toward my high school graduation requirements. Perhaps they questioned the educational stringency when my grade in French (a language where I could only say "hello" and "I am a little notebook") was higher than my grade in English.

Steve and I were now in the same academic year and would be graduating from high school together. Life had given us another playing field to compete on, though Steve had tapped out of the competition against me long ago. Beating me carried no weight for him. He was secure in knowing that my mom loved him regardless. I don't know what he felt inside growing up, but I doubt it was the level of shame and fear of inadequacy that consumed me by the time I was in high school.

I sought tangible ways to measure myself against others, and class rank was one of those. When I left for Bolivia at the beginning of my sophomore year, I was positioned in the 11th spot out of hundreds of students. Upon my return to the U.S. and entry to my brother's grade, my rank shot up to fourth. It was then that the old standardized-test-score obsession of mine boiled to the surface. It made sense now. I had finally cracked the reason why he was considered "gifted and talented," and I got Average Jill status. His class was less academically competitive than mine. My scores never changed, but when I was switched to his grade level, my rank improved because the competition was not as stiff. It was an ugly feeling of smug satisfaction, knowing that I would have been good enough for the gifted and talented program. I was just in the wrong year.

In hindsight, I wish I could have let the fixation on the test score go. I wish in my childhood I could have just been happy for Steve. I wish I could have understood what was driving me to crave success and winning. I wish I could have verbalized the feelings of despair and shame I felt for not being perfect in everything. But admitting those feelings would have meant admitting that I wasn't perfect.

To this day, I wonder what drove me toward wanting to achieve Star Baby status in every aspect of my life. I know that I wanted to please my mom. She poured herself into motherhood, and I wanted to reciprocate the love I felt by showing her I could be the best daughter possible. She sacrificed aspects of her life by becoming a mother, and I wanted to show her that I could achieve the dreams that she was not afforded the opportunity to chase.

I also felt a responsibility to myself. I confused perfectionism with having high self-esteem, when the truth was actually the opposite. I needed perfectionism to make me feel worthy. Perfectionism meant that others showered me with praise and acceptance, complete external validation that I had purpose. Rather than feeling loved for who I was, I became accustomed to feeling loved for what I accomplished—an empty and fleeting kind of love.

One thing I've learned is that God, or Source, or the Universe, whatever you prefer to call your creator, has an interesting sense of humor. My mom wanted me to be Star Baby. She knew I would achieve something great in life, though she didn't know what.

HOLDING HANDS

The ground seemed unstable, and I felt like I was gulping air on occasion. Normal breathing was difficult. Altitude sickness was beginning to set in. I ambled along the cocoa-colored dusty ground, teetering to one side or another. She slid her soft, delicate right hand into my left and held it as we walked the remainder of the way. I found breathing more difficult for a different reason now.

I was new to Cochabamba, Bolivia. This kicked off my year as a Rotary Youth Exchange student in the other half of the world. I was 15 years old and desperate to go anywhere that wasn't my hometown in Western New York. I remember landing and it being the first time I had ever gotten off a plane that wasn't connected to a gate. That felt exhilarating to me. I had done it. Escaped suburban, middle-class life for a chance at the unknown.

That's when I met my host sister for the year. Carolina was beautiful, not that I viewed her in an attraction sort of way at that time. She was just beautiful by our traditional standards of beauty: tall and fit, with long, thick, jet-black hair, naturally tanned unblemished skin, and rich brown eyes that looked like morning coffee with a drop of cream. She didn't wear makeup. She wasn't overly fussy about her hair, which always had a wave in it from when she'd put it in a messy knot on the back of her head. She moved with the confidence of the medal-winning track star that she was, but also with a soft grace at the times when teenage bouts of shyness crept in.

She made me nervous for reasons that I didn't understand. I know. I was 15. I should have understood. But up until that point, my exposure to relationships and feelings of attraction was mostly unknown. At that age, my friend group had turned into little more than the peers I saw in my classroom, at after-school clubs, or on the swim team. I was so busy with extracurriculars and hanging out with my mom, that I skipped the step where you're supposed to have boy talk with your girlfriends, go to parties, and experiment in some basement closet for seven agonizing minutes. Instead, I was driven to build an enviable résumé, while simultaneously trying to figure out why I felt like a space alien in my hometown. All I knew in that moment was that I liked looking at Carolina and being around her energy.

When she held my hand that first day as she showed me around the school campus, my first reaction was internal panic. Why was she touching me? Did that mean she liked me? More importantly, what if someone saw us? What would they think about us? There was nobody around us, and yet in that moment I felt like there were eyes everywhere burning into me for what I was engaged in. This wasn't right. Good girls don't do this.

I was raised in what was considered a "not homophobic" household. We knew single gay men and gay couples, and we were cool with them because they were always so nice to us. They felt safe to my mom, and later to me. We loved the people they were and the security they gave us in knowing that we couldn't possibly be homophobic with them as friends. What they did with their partners and every aspect of their private lives remained behind closed doors, just where we felt comfortable with it. No hand-holding, gentle caressing, or even quick kissing ever occurred. I'm not sure if that's because it would have felt like too much for them to do in public back in the early '90s, when the stigma around gay men and the fear of AIDS was rampant across the U.S. Or maybe they did it for our comfort, knowing that we were okay allowing them to exist but not quite comfortable enough to let them openly be who they were.

These feelings arose in me again as Carolina took my hand. Even though there was nothing sexual or romantic about it, my body couldn't shake the feeling coursing through me that this was somehow wrong. The fact that I liked it made it feel even more wrong. It never dawned on me that the "wrongness" I felt had been from my own cultural and societal conditioning. At the time, I would have never viewed these feelings as being homophobic.

I was going to need some mental gymnastics to be okay with this one. My mind flipped back to some middle school Spanish textbook that taught us how Latin cultures were more affectionate than my white American life. In Latin America people might greet each other with a kiss on the cheek and possibly a hug. Girls might hold hands with their friend. I allowed myself permission to keep holding Carolina's hand because the textbook told me it was okay. *This was cultural,* I told myself. Nothing more. Nothing wrong. Even still, my nervous insides were waiting for it to end.

She let go of my hand to open the old wooden door of our classroom and I gulped in a breath of relief. My hypervigilance that someone would see us and think something negative about us began to subside. We could go back to just being girls hanging out together. The reality is, that's all we were anyway. I brought my attention back to the simple classroom with bare plaster walls, one row of windows, and a chalkboard at the front. It was a stark contrast to the colorfully postered U.S. classrooms I was used to. There were three rows of wooden desks with two-seater benches at each one. I wondered who I would get paired up with for the coming school year. Everything felt so new and slightly overwhelming. I let out a deep exhale at the realization that there would be a lot of new and overwhelming experiences over the course of the next year. This was only day one.

We left the school campus and dodged city traffic in a roundabout that had a statue of a revolutionary hero, assault weapon raised in triumph over his head as he knelt on the ground. Carolina and I walked swiftly back to the Chinese restaurant where my entire extended host family was eager to meet and surround me with conversation that I didn't yet understand. I waited and hoped during that walk that she would take my hand again.

HARD-COPY FACEBOOK AND A MISLEADING HAIRCUT

Teenage years are brutal. Acne and physical awkwardness aside, the teenage years become an emotional battleground for the person you are inside and the way the world perceives you. You're called on to show maturity, when emotionally you still want to play on the swings. You're supposed to start planning your educational and career future, when just a short while ago you could barely make yourself a sandwich. You watch your friends rapidly grow and change at different rates and wonder what happened to the friendships that seemed so unbreakable just a few years prior, when you knotted friendship bracelets and exchanged necklace halves. You start to wonder about changes within yourself and how the people around you view the person you're becoming.

I never shared with anyone the feelings I had when I held another girl's hand. Why would I, really? It was never going to be a question that was ever asked of me, particularly not back in the mid-'90s when the only people who seemed to be gay were men or Ellen DeGeneres. Asking a child if they were queer was not something parents did back then. (Heck, it's hardly something many parents think to ask now!) Regardless, I refused to admit that what I felt might be attraction. I refused to admit it even to myself. I couldn't separate the excitement of holding her hand from the overwhelming paranoia that I was doing something wrong. All I knew at that age was that if something felt wrong, regardless of how exciting it was, it was probably wrong. I packed the memory away.

My lack of interest in others didn't go unnoticed. Most of the time I could deflect inquiries about my lack of interest in dating, claiming it was due to my laser-like focus on my future. I would tell people that I didn't have time for dating. I buried my suspicions under a heap of stories that something might be wrong with me for not being wildly attracted to boys: They're too immature for me. I'm too busy for them. Nobody is an intellectual match for me at this age.

My favorite story that I used to tell myself was that I was just an atypical teenager, easily escaping my peers' downfalls of being "boy crazy" or "promiscuous." I prided myself on apparently skipping the stage in development when I was supposed to abandon common sense and rational thought for the hormonal whims of being 16. Take *that,* underdeveloped prefrontal cortex! I've outwitted you and human biology.

My mom was proud of my achievements as well and mostly supported my narrative that I was goal oriented. She seemed to understand that because dating offered no gold stars, it held no value to me. So when she sat me down in the living room one day, I was caught off guard. Perhaps she was seeking a moment that felt like mother-daughter bonding to her. Gossipy. Vulnerable. Friend-like. Asking her about that day now, she claims no recollection of it. What was a vivid memory for me was innocuously pruned from her brain decades ago as an unnecessary item to store. What felt big to me felt ordinary to her.

There she and I sat on our knees, side by side on the hunter-green carpet of the living room in my childhood home with my school yearbook in front of us. Tufts of blond dog hair collected in corners and around our boxy TV that was equal parts furniture and electronics. My eyes meandered from the tufts to the small, gray rectangles with the faces of my high school classmates.

"What about him?" she asked, pointing to a picture of a guy named Derek.

"No," I said shyly. I was immediately uncomfortable with this game that could have been titled "Find Jill a Boyfriend or Risk Painful Death by 1,000 Yearbook Papercuts." There were approximately 444 people in my class at that time. Once you narrowed down the male population and factored out the stoners and loners, approximately 212 of them were prime for the lusting. Except, unlike dating apps, the pool of applicants hadn't thrown their name in the ring as eligible bachelors. They were just being evaluated because they went to school with me. Essentially, it was hard-copy Facebook. My mom invented hard-copy Facebook before Mark Zuckerberg decided to move it to an electronic tool to evaluate chicks in his school.

"What about him?" Her eyebrows raised in hope as her manicured nail pointed at a jock named Mike.

"Mmmm mmmm," I groaned as I shook my head from side to side. Even if I found him attractive, which I didn't, I was consciously aware that we were in different dating leagues.

She picked up the yearbook off the floor and examined the faces a bit closer. I became aware of my brother lingering while perusing the snack cabinet in our kitchen, a smirk on his face as he grabbed a pack of Fig Newtons.

"Jim's cute! He's smart too, right?"

"He's dating someone," I deflected.

"Whatever happened to Matt. You liked him back in elementary school, remember?" She scrolled through the alphabetical index of names to find the boy who came to a pool party at my house one day when I was in the fifth grade. "Oh my . . . he didn't age well, huh?"

I just shook my head.

Both of our frustrations were growing now. I felt bad for my mom. Her bonding moment had gone awry. I couldn't tell if she was disappointed that the outcome was not as she hoped it would be, or if she felt concern that something was wrong with me for not wanting to date as a teenager. For me, it's the first memory I can recall of feeling broken. I was not right. Something was wrong with me because I didn't feel the way I was supposed to feel. While I strived to maintain control in every aspect of my life, my internal feelings were not something I had dominion over. This became my secret to keep.

The term *asexual* wasn't in my vernacular back then, but I wondered if there were people out there like me who just didn't feel attraction. In my heteronormative world, not being attracted to guys meant to me that I wasn't attracted to anyone. I hoped that maybe things would get better once I got to the college dating pool, where I would be in a larger pond with those of similar interests and intellectual capabilities. I held out hope that someday I'd feel the kind of attraction to men that I saw on TV shows and in the movies. For the time being, in my high school years, I just wanted to focus on getting A's, running every club, and winning medals.

"Now *he's* attractive," Mom exclaimed in a last-ditch effort. She gestured toward a face with delicate features and a neat, white-blond crop of hair. "What's his name?" she asked as she ran her finger excitedly toward the alphabetical names. I beat her to the punch.

"Becky."

In the kitchen, Steve lost himself in laughter.

PRUDES AND JOHNS

Every time I share with someone in my current life that I dated not one but several boys in my youth, I feel like a lesbian in a rehab meeting admitting my missteps and wrongdoing. I envisioned myself twisting my body up like an uncomfortable pretzel seated on a metal folding chair, sipping some stale, dust-flavored coffee from a paper cup, and confessing that it's been X number of days since my last heterosexual relationship. Sometimes in my current life, there are those who attempt to invalidate my identity as a lesbian because of my relationship history. People call them *gatekeepers*, without realizing there is no gate to keep. While outwardly laws and societal behaviors can influence how I carry myself, there is nobody who can prevent me from knowing my true self. My identity is not up for debate. Nobody's identity is up for debate. And my dating history, viewed from the glorious vantage point of hindsight, offered some revealing details as to why the issues of sexual identity and attraction are so confusing.

The first time I got called a *prude* I thought they had called me a *prune*. I was in fifth grade. The concept of prudish behavior was as foreign to me as when a sushi place opened in my pizza- and wings-loving hometown of Buffalo, New York.

I recall flipping open the dark blue cover of my family's heavy dictionary and finding the word *prude*, "a person who is or claims to be easily shocked by matters related to sex or nudity." I'm sure I slammed the book shut as soon as my eyes reached the end of the definition. I'm sure I blushed at just reading the words *sex* and *nudity*. Just *thinking* those words felt inappropriate at that stage of my development. Sex and the human body were not areas that my family or I showed comfort with. Perhaps that is why I didn't feel any strong emotions about being called a prude. It was the truth—or at least closer to the truth than my being a prune.

That was the lesson I learned from my less-than-two-week fifth-grade courtship with a boy named John. He was a drummer. He played street hockey. He had pegs on the back wheel of his bike. He seemed cool. But more importantly, my friend had a crush on him, so he must have been cool. Suddenly, dating John became a goal to achieve. I don't recall being asked out by him, just a mutual understanding that we would be going to Ponderosa's all-you-can-eat buffet together to celebrate the end of elementary school with some other members of our class. While he didn't let me ride on the pegs of his bike to the restaurant, by the time my friends and I arrived on foot, I found that he had saved me a seat. How utterly romantic.

I do remember thinking John was cute to look at. I don't remember wanting to do anything else with him. I do remember that saying we were dating, though, made me feel like I had leveled up socially, as I inched my way closer to what the cool kids were doing. There it was at the ripe age of 11, a sense that there were things I should be doing and should be wanting with boys.

Society sent signals and I received them loud and clear. This is how a girl is supposed to behave. This is what a girl is supposed to want. This is how boys want girls to behave, which often seemed in opposition to how society wanted girls to behave. Be *this* if you want to attract a mate, but also don't because it's not ladylike. Perhaps life would have been less complicated if I were a prune.

And so, within two weeks after our initial date, I was approached by a neighborhood girl on a bicycle, who informed me that she was dating John now and that he had broken up with me because I was a prude. I shrugged my shoulders and went back to trying to ride a unicycle like the happily, single weirdo I was.

My slow climb to the top of elementary school popularity took a sharp dive through my middle school and high school years, as I craved the touch of a book in my hands over that of another human. Whenever I lifted my head out of the pages for moments of socialization, I found myself being pressured back into the dating scene. This happened one evening during my year abroad in Bolivia at a small house party at my friend's apartment while her parents were out of town. At some point in the evening, I remember looking around and realizing that nearly everyone in attendance had paired off with someone else. Juan was my friend's older brother. Allegedly, he was studying to be a doctor. I weighed the benefit of fitting in at that party with the cost of having to admit to my mother that I was dating someone a few years older than me. I figured his solid educational path would probably be seen as a win by her. He was probably the kind of guy I was supposed to be dating. I looked into his eyes, trying to light a fire of attraction within myself. With his shaved head and oversized Adam's apple, I couldn't wipe the image of the Looney Tunes buzzard from my mind. I hoped our intellectual connection might be enough instead.

Juan was my first kiss. I knew it was coming that evening at the party, just moments after he asked me if I wanted to go out with him. We were sitting on the floor in the dark, surrounded by couples in their own states of romantic embrace. Instead, my body shook. It was a small tremble at first, crescendoing into more violent shakes when I felt his lips press against my tightly closed mouth. I remember thinking, *So this is kissing?* and wondering why people enjoyed it so much. He kept asking if I was cold, apparently thinking my body was overcome by shivers. To me, my insides felt like they were under assault from Ping-Pong balls bouncing off every corner of me as I tried to make sense of what was going on. Did I like what we were doing? Was this nervous excitement? Did I want it to just end and the lights to turn on and to go home and curl up in my bed alone? What did my friends think of me?

The feeling never went away. Every time we tried to kiss, my body would start to shake and the tension would be palpable in every cell. Within two weeks, Juan called it quits. I felt relief.

As my high school graduation approached, I looked back on my teen years and realized that I had achieved nearly every goal I set for myself and would soon be on my way to Boston University with a full scholarship. My future seemed bright, but there was that small shadow within me that realized that my pursuits of excellence had kept me from experiencing what it was to be a teenager.

Like the baby that goes from sitting to walking, completely skipping the crawling stage, perhaps I had missed an important developmental step. I didn't experiment with cigarettes or drugs. I didn't experiment with touching anyone of any gender. The wildest I went was dyeing my hair nearly black and getting a pixie cut in an attempt to look like Winona Ryder. She was cool and edgy. One of my friends told me, instead, that my new cut reminded her of our seventh-grade English teacher. Not the look I was going for.

It was the closest I had ever come to wanting to be rebellious. With my future secured, I felt like I had now earned the right to test waters and explore why my teenager switch was never flipped to the on position. I tried dating one co-worker from my job at the laser tag arena. He left me halfway through our first date at a concert to go make out with a girl from his high school. Apparently, I was too much of a prune for him. I dated another one of my laser tag co-workers because he was very much interested in me and had the added bonus of having his own car and apartment. We watched *Top Gun* and made out a lot, with far fewer bodily convulsions than I felt during my first kiss in Bolivia. I wondered if kissing was supposed to be so slobbery. But I was into it. He had a bit of a bad-guy vibe and I liked how it juxtaposed with my straight-laced life. His eyes were nice, which helped me overlook his widespread cystic acne. I knew we didn't have a future together, with me going away to college, and I had no problem walking away when that time came. He was like that slightly unsafe carnival ride, providing a brief adrenaline rush while also leading you to question when the ride would be over so you could try something new.

This dating experience seemed to overlap with another guy (also named John) whom my mom wanted me to date . . . also from the laser tag arena. He was everything a parent wants in their daughter's partner: smart, nice, respectful, and male. And he really, really wanted to go out with me. My mom begged me to date John when he offered to take me to a comedy show. I complied, because that's who I was, and I really, really tried to make myself feel something for him. But wishing attraction doesn't make it happen, no matter how much sense someone seems to make on paper. I had no lukewarm feelings toward him, and with each kind gesture I felt like I was taking advantage of him. There was never going to be anything between us, no matter how much he or my mom wanted there to be.

I was henceforth banned from the laser tag arena.

College was the opportunity to start over and correct the pieces of my identity that I felt I had failed at as a teen. Nobody knew me here. Nobody knew I was a prude. But being at college also meant I could no longer hide behind the narrative that I just wasn't surrounded by intellectual males "of my level" like in high school. Here, I was a small, smart fish in a large pond of smart fish. I hoped that the story I had told myself and others was true. I really hoped I could find a man that I could connect with, feel safe with, and be attracted to. I hoped his name wouldn't be John or Juan, based on my string of unfortunate luck with that name.

He wasn't a John. He was a Chris. And he was tan, had gorgeous blue eyes, and a scruffy goatee. He was from Miami, and my sheltered instincts assumed he was a drug dealer. Why else would anyone leave the sunny South except to sell drugs to the many rich New Englanders who populated our school? He wasn't a drug dealer, though.

He wasn't a drug user either. In fact, he was an insanely interesting and sweet guy. We shared stories of our time abroad—his in Spain playing soccer and mine in Bolivia attending high school and volunteering at an orphanage. I knew from the beginning that something was different about Chris. His personality was magnetic. Everyone wanted to be around him. He was funny, grinned a lot, and treated everyone like a best friend. When my mom and I crossed paths with him and his family during Parents Weekend at Boston University, she asked, "Who's that?" I told her that he lived on my floor. "You should go out with him," she responded. Matchmaker Mom was at it again, and this time I felt like I could give it a go.

This is where looking back in hindsight gets confusing. I can say without any doubt in my mind that I was attracted to Chris. I loved to look at his face. I liked his broad shoulders and how I felt safe and protected when he wrapped me in his arms. I didn't recoil at his touch, like I had with other guys, and appreciated the fact that he was willing to take things slow. Despite his cool and personable exterior, it turned out that we were both inexperienced and had limited dating history. If there was a dating checklist for compatibility, Chris would have checked all the boxes. Finally, it seemed, I had achieved the one aspect of being a human that had evaded me for so long—I had found a mate.

Perhaps I was heterosexual. Perhaps I was bisexual. Perhaps I was attracted to him on the level I needed to be to carry on a romantic relationship. Perhaps I didn't know who I was except that I wanted to be with him and he was something special. I remember on our first date, in a tiny basement restaurant called Deli Haus, that our conversation flowed easily and quickly took a deep dive into what we wanted our futures to look like. I marveled at how comfortable he seemed in sharing his desires to eventually have a family with lots of soccer-playing children. I bristled at the thought of sharing with him that marriage and children of my own had never been on my radar. In fact, my mom had bet me at some point in high school that if I was married by the time I was 30, I would have to take her to Hawaii. If I wasn't married, she would take me. I was confident that I would win that bet. I hoped it wasn't a problem that I wasn't the type of girl who dreamed of her future wedding. My heart was calling me to be wild and join the Peace Corps after college, to travel abroad and care for all of the babies that were not my own. Despite these long-range differences, Chris and I persevered. What we had in our relationship felt good to us.

We spent all four years of college together with nary a spat or threat of breakup. We were each other's first serious relationship and were in it for the long haul. Finally, I thought I had found what everyone was always seeking—a partner who was a best friend. Finally, I could fulfill the role of womanhood that seemed to evade me for so long.

ORPHANS AND AUDITORS

As I prepared to graduate from college, I felt like I had achieved the pinnacle of "Supposed To" mountain. I was supposed to graduate from a prestigious university with highest honors on my diploma. I was supposed to get a good-paying, respectable corporate job with a well-known firm. I was supposed to settle down with a kind man who loved me deeply. Pride oozed from my pores. My future looked bright and organized. The pieces of my life were falling together in the most perfect manner. If this had been *The Game of Life,* I was winning, just like I was supposed to.

One of the final stages to exiting Boston University's Questrom School of Business was to have an interview with a faculty member or local business leader about where life would take me once outside of the brick university walls. My discussion would take place within the bustling Starbucks that had been built on the second floor of our business school. As I approached the table, an older gentleman presented his hand and smiled. I shook it and gracefully lowered myself into the chair with as much poise and confidence as I could muster. Things were off to a solid start.

"So," he began, "if you could do anything in this world, tell me what your dream job would be."

My solid start was gone. Things crumbled quickly once his words began. I had already planned this conversation in my mind before the interview. He would ask me about my career plans. I would dazzle him with my list of collegiate accomplishments and my smooth road to becoming a certified public accountant. He would pat me on the back and say, "Attagirl!" I would smile back politely and thank him for his time.

He clearly did not read the playbook in my mind. Hopes and dreams had no place in this conversation. The track had been set over the past several years and I had too much momentum to stop my train. This would have been a better conversation as a freshman or as a four-year-old, I thought. Not now. Back then was the time for hope and dreams. Now my focus was on doing what was right and best. I had convinced myself that hopes and dreams were for the misguided anyway, those with their heads in the clouds who only wished for a good life. Not me. I was practical and grounded firmly in achievement. I was going to make my good life.

I let the coffee-scented air enter my lungs as far as my tight rib cage would allow. My brain was angry. My lungs burned. I let out a deep exhale, and with it went some of my judgment and expectation. And then, for a moment I felt relief. What if I allowed myself a little vacation to just dream again? After so many years with my feet firmly on the ground and my gaze straight ahead, it might be nice to play in the "what if"s. This was the first conversation I had

had in a while with someone who wasn't looking for me to give the correct answer or the best answer, just an honest answer. I felt the words rise from my heart space instead of down from my brain.

"Honestly . . ." I paused, waiting for any signal that something other than honesty was what he was looking for. A smile crept across my face, "I would love to work with orphaned and abandoned infants again like I did during my year abroad in Bolivia. I would love to come up with a program that would provide them with the holding and touch they need to be able to bond and create healthy brain development." I didn't wait for his reaction, and my answer turned into a heartfelt ramble about my experience holding these orphaned and abandoned babies and the disconnect I saw in most of their eyes. I had always dreamed that if I just had more time or could engage more people, we could hold the babies more and build that connection again through the power of therapeutic touch. If I could be there for them, it might change the course of their lives in a significant way. The thought of affecting positive change in others filled me from head to toe. My heart felt warm. My eyes probably twinkled. I may have even levitated two inches from my chair with the lightness of my energy.

He picked up my résumé and gave it a once-over while leaning back in his chair.

"Hmmm," he said.

The weight of the pause energetically brought me back into my chair. The burning sensation returned to my lungs. I held my breath waiting for the next beat. I could tell he was searching for the right words. I hoped they would be kind.

Instead, they were honest. "How do you plan on doing that by becoming an accountant?"

It was a valid question that felt like a pin to the balloon that was my perfectionist ego. In that moment, I realized that all of the hard work I had put into studying a subject that I didn't find interesting but had a talent for, all of the time I spent tutoring other accounting students to strengthen my knowledge of the material, all of the hours I spent volunteering as a tax consultant so that my résumé would seem more well-rounded, all of the classes that I forced myself to pay attention to while feeling jealous of my classmates who got to study more exciting subjects like marketing and organizational behavior, all of the accounting internships I tried to feign excitement and pride for, all of the things I had invested my energy in over the past four years—they were all just to meet the expectations of what I thought people wanted of me. Now I was being asked what I wanted to do, what I truly wanted to do, and it didn't line up. The pride of accomplishing my parents' dream (and what I thought was also my dream) suddenly felt shallow.

My ego stepped in to rescue me from this realization. It reminded me that those passion paths were not real. People didn't *really* live that way. If my dream was possible to achieve, then someone would have done it already. Dreaming was for children who didn't need responsibility and adults with no direction. I told myself that adults with the biggest dreams were the ones who ended up working low-paying, low-satisfaction jobs because they kept their heads in the clouds instead of focused on the practical road ahead.

I wondered at what point in my youth I began to believe that "you can be whatever you want when you grow up" was a lie. I didn't know anyone who actually lived that way. Everyone, including my parents, seemed to just keep putting one foot in front of the other, trudging on to their next required step. If this was living, I wondered why people lived. I felt no more alive taking my next required step than a cog in a machine feels as it makes its next forced rotation. At least my steps as a CPA would get me prestige and stability. I'd get a solid paycheck. I'd work in a gray plastic cubicle at a gray table with a dark-gray cushioned chair. It would probably be ergonomically correct. I didn't deserve to feel upset. What I had was what other people envied. What I had was good enough.

My dream career, conversely, had no direction, no structure, no outcome, and no income. It would feel greedy and selfish to do what I wanted to do. It was unstable to do what others had not done. It might fail and that would make me reliant on others for survival. I told myself that dream career just didn't have a place here on Earth.

But deep down I was upset. I knew that for everything that could go wrong in my dream career, I was only given one shot at this life. My heart hurt to know that I had positioned myself on the life path that would never get me to the work that spoke to my heart. It was time to cross that dream job off my dream list.

Dreams were reserved for things that still seemed somewhat achievable, if we worked or prayed hard enough or got lucky enough. As hard as I tried, I couldn't come up with a single way to connect the dots between becoming an auditor and transitioning to a child caretaker in an overseas orphanage. My life's dream had now been moved to the shelf of impossibility, all while sipping a cup of acrid coffee. My brain told my heart to just forget about it. I had spent the past four years and hundreds of thousands of scholarship dollars to become an accountant. Too much had already been invested in my path.

That day, I packed up my soul's yearning, grabbed my laptop, and convinced myself that my only option was to trudge forward with a proud face into my respectable future as a financial statement auditor. There was no room left for dreaming.

Too much time had been invested. It was too late to change.

PICTURE-PERFECT WEDDING

If there is one thing I have specialized in for most of my adult life, it's awkwardly uncomfortable interactions with my future in-laws. From our first encounter, when I oddly served myself a slab of Sasquatch-portioned steak because I was too nervous to cut it into a smaller piece (and risk offending their generous Hispanic food offering), to that moment when, surrounded by aunts, uncles, and cousins, it became obvious that someone had spilled the frijoles about Chris and I living together unmarried. *Painful* became the best adjective to describe my relationship with most of his family.

This did not improve with time, nor did the abnormal number of cheesy jokes that I threw at every situation to try and ease the tension and appear witty. So, when Chris proposed to me after six years of smooth and argument-free dating, I hoped that the knowledge of our future family union would warm the frigid air between me and nearly everyone else on his side.

Hope. If there's one thing I've learned about myself it's that I am an endless fountain of unsubstantiated and baseless hope.

"So, what kind of wedding dress do you want?" one of the aunts asked as we sat around a table at the fine dining establishment of McDonald's. It was summertime and Chris and I ventured from Florida to South Carolina to visit his extended family and share the good news of our recent engagement and commitment to no longer living together in sin. While the men were off doing manly things, I took the unwanted spotlight among the table of future female relatives. As per usual, my mind could barely string together a coherent sentence in its awkward tug-of-war attempt to sound like the ideal addition to their family.

It was that question of the dress, though, that got me because I realized that I had never thought about what kind of wedding dress I would wear . . . never. I meandered down the mental pathway of realizing that, although we had been dating for six years and, although I assumed marriage was in our future, I had never actually thought about our wedding.

I stammered out the most intelligent-sounding "Uhhh" as I grabbed a few more salty fries and wished they were already blocking sounds from coming out of my face. "I guess probably a halter," I added. "Because, you know, I don't really have much of anything on top," I so eloquently added while motioning to the location where womanly breasts should have sprouted in my teenage years. My brain pounced back into self-judgment mode as I questioned why a halter was the only obvious neckline choice for the small-chested, and I plowed the fries into my face to stop the talking. Everyone else filled their mouths with fries too.

Our wedding day was magazine-perfect: from the Miami rooftop reception and the dulce de leche–filled cake to the merengue band and painted Dominican espresso cups that everyone received as a parting gift. Over 100 guests danced the night away, including my family members from Buffalo, who soaked in the warm temperatures on that January night so far from their home.

That wedding was how so many people envision their weddings. Lively. Classy. Fun. That wedding was everything except a representation of me. That's nobody's fault, either, but my own. That's just what happens when (1) you have no vision for what you think your day should look like, (2) you have no voice to express how you feel, and (3) you have no identity, except for the fact that you've always been a good student and are now a good CPA working for a good firm. People-pleasing had become my second full-time job.

Clad in my unofficial uniform of khaki pants and pastel sweater sets, I was living the American dream of working a corporate job and living in a townhouse in my deed-restricted community with my college sweetheart. We earned good money. We traveled when we wanted to. We had friends. What else could either of us possibly want? What else could we even ask for?

PAYCHECKS AND PICKUP TRUCKS

It was the end of another 80-hour workweek. My already slim frame was 10 pounds lighter from surviving off Reese's Peanut Butter Cups and endless mugs of Splenda-sweetened coffee. I looked more like a wire clothes hanger for my suit than a human filling it out. My hair was starting to fall out.

I was grateful for the day our managing partner gave us half a Friday off as reward for meeting the filing deadline. Oh, what to do with these hours of newly found freedom? I drove to a massage therapy school. I didn't want a massage; I wanted to enroll.

After several years in and many tears, I realized what a mismatch auditing was for my skills and personality. I could do the work. I didn't enjoy the work. It paid the bills and was respectable. I hated life. "But look toward the future," people would remind me. "You could be a partner in thirteen years!" That was not a goal that enticed or satisfied me in the least, aside from the title and paycheck.

This was my first big leap into doing something that felt more like me. It was terrifying and I was quietly judged by family members behind my back. I would learn of their disappointment through gossip. I hoped, like the game of *Telephone,* that maybe they were just slightly proud and that the message got twisted along the way. I was also beginning to not care as much either. I wanted my hair to grow back.

It's funny that I don't recall how my mind made the change from certified public accountant to licensed massage therapist. It was the about-face, career wise, that nobody saw coming. They couldn't believe I would give up on the solid career that I had already invested so much time in. People couldn't understand why I would throw away my CPA license when I had worked so hard to get it. They couldn't see that license as the shackle on my leg that I could drag around for the rest of my life, or cut my losses and free myself from its weight.

Perhaps the bigger shock to everyone was that I would give up the pride associated with the title of CPA for the questionable reception I would get from people when I announced I was a massage therapist. This would be a big shift in my identity and how others viewed me. The usual "Wow!"s I got with my old job would be replaced with crude jokes about "happy endings" and rubbing people down with oil for money. They didn't understand, but I didn't need them to. This was my life that I had to live each day.

Here I was, still in my corporate suit, driving my car over to a massage school for a tour and to find out their next enrollment date. I figured that maybe after graduating I could open my own massage business. Maybe I could even have some people work for me. Perhaps I could do work I loved *and* still feel like my business degree wasn't for naught. At the very least, I knew a slew of stressed-out accountants who could use a good therapeutic massage. My transition made sense to me, though most others couldn't understand it.

I had always found myself drawn to bodywork throughout my youth. Sometime in elementary school I bought a book from Barnes & Noble about reflexology, the ancient art of foot massage. It was quite clearly over my head in terms of comprehension, but I followed the guide in the book of how to perform a reflexology routine and what to palpate for, and used my mom as a very willing client. Later, I bought a book called *The Power of Your Subconscious Mind* by Joseph Murphy. Again, the content was beyond my level of comprehension, and I struggled to make it through the chapters with any sort of understanding. My takeaway, though, was that life, health, and our bodies were far more complex than my fifth-grade science book led us to believe.

The many months between the time I enrolled in massage school that Friday in February and when my class started in October seemed to fly by in a blur. My entire focus was on my new life. I found myself daydreaming more about the direction I was headed and what this new life could be like for me. I imagined myself feeling healthy again and feeding my body the food and water it needed. I envisioned helping others reduce pain and taking care of my family members so that they didn't have to hurt. And I imagined wearing lots of linen pants. Oh, to be in soft, flowing clothes every day and smell like sandalwood. I painted a picture of my new life so vividly in my mind that I couldn't imagine it not happening.

Our massage class was relatively small—fewer than 20 students from all different walks of life. Some were kids fresh out of high school whose parents told them to pick a job. One was a guy who encouraged us all to buy gold bars and not give the government our fingerprints. One was a kind, 50-something Canadian woman who had recently moved to Florida for her husband's work. She had been a craniosacral therapy (CST) practitioner for years and just wanted to continue her practice in her new home state. And then there was Amy.

Amy was in every way my opposite—the yang to my yin. There was a softness and blandness to the way I dressed and acted. Her black tank tops, studded belt, and black hair, styled in a faux hawk, felt hard. She swore. She made inappropriate jokes. There was something about her that scared me. I was vanilla. She was rocky road.

But when it came to treating a client on the table, she demonstrated her skill as an intuitive and talented therapist. The perfectionist in me liked people who were good at what they did. I was determined to make her my friend. It was truly unfortunate that she did not share the same goal.

One morning, only a few days into our new massage therapy journey, I was outside in the parking lot, grabbing my books and sheets out of the trunk of my car. I looked up as a horn blared and saw Amy peel into the parking lot in her old, black pickup truck, with another truck in pursuit behind her still laying on the horn. She parked abruptly and got out of her truck. A burly man rolled out of the other truck.

"Fucking bitch! You cut me off! What the hell were you doing?"

"Sir," she said in a slow Southern drawl from her Georgia upbringing, her hands going up in front of her in apologetic defense. "It was an accident. I apologize."

"You almost caused a fucking accident! Bitch."

"Sir, you have your son in the car. We're all okay. Please just get back in your truck. Okay? I'm sorry." I saw her try to muster a reassuring smile to the little boy in the truck, while attempting to tame his hotheaded parent.

I watched in frozen horror from the sidelines as he flung insult after expletive her way. My own insides screamed at me: *Say something! Do something!* My courage didn't extend that far though. I felt hopeless as I saw her withstand the verbal assault, wishing I had been as brave and strong as I liked to pretend I was in my mind. When it came down to it, though, I was scared stiff and ashamed of it. My whole life I had perfected the art of staying out of things that weren't my business. Not causing trouble. Not getting involved. Staying in my lane.

Although Amy had a quiver in her voice, I marveled at her strength. She stood her ground with composure, not aggression. She did everything to calm the situation. I wondered where her strength came from. Had she been through this before? People verbalizing hateful words her way, and her having to deflect and defuse? I could feel that she was bothered on the inside, but would be damned if she gave any indication of that on the outside.

The man climbed back in his truck and slammed the door. He leaned his head out the window as he pulled away. "Fucking DYKE!" was heard loud and clear by the growing crowd of students that had arrived and were ready to start the day. That last verbal dagger hit her. I could see a pain in her face. I watched Amy put up an invisible shield of armor as she grabbed her supplies, avoided eye contact, and headed into the building.

As we sat in our class that morning, tables shaped in a U, with Amy seated at the bottom of the curve and me at the top left, she asked our teacher if she could take a moment to address the class. She apologized for the scene in the parking lot that morning. Some classmates consoled her that it wasn't her fault and there was no need to apologize. I agreed, but I felt frozen again and not sure of the right words to say. So I said nothing. She didn't strike me as the type of person who was looking for hugs. I just stared like I was a weird baby deer and let the classmates nearest to her offer support.

And then she said it. "I am a lesbian," Amy told the class. Time froze. I had not pieced together that when the man called her a *dyke* that she could actually, truly, in fact be a gay person. And here she was, announcing it so easily and with no apparent trepidation. My brain couldn't compute what I had just heard. "I just moved here to live with my girlfriend and we're very happy together. There was no reason for him to call me that name."

While the class moved on, my mind was still stuck on *lesbian*. It was not the first time I had heard the word out loud, but it felt like it was. A foreign sound to my virgin ears. Maybe because it was the first time I had heard a lesbian *identify* herself as a lesbian. Maybe it was also because it was the first time I recall hearing the word not used as a slur or a tease. *Lesbian* wasn't being used to describe someone in gossip. Amy used it like it was any old, run-of-the-mill adjective instead of a charged word, like *fuck* or *Voldemort*, that one should only utter in the most necessary of circumstances.

It was a strange and vivid moment for me. Lesbians did exist and I was now in the presence of a real one.

BLOODSUCKERS AND MUSTANGS

"You have really nice arm muscles. Do you lift weights?"

Yes, that was my awkward segue into approaching Amy, my newfound real-life lesbian. She was fascinating to me. While I'd love to use the poetic cliché of being drawn to her like a moth to a flame, it was really more like me being a life-sucking mosquito attracted to the blue-lighted bug zapper that was her. *How could it hurt me? It's so glowing and radiant!* I told myself.

She adjusted the black baseball cap on her head and responded with a curt, "It's from my job." I bobbed my head like it was filled with air, which it may have been because no additional thoughts came to my mind as I awkwardly slinked away. Outside of the glow of her blue light, my mind could reengage and come up with a laundry list of additional questions. It was as if I had forgotten how to carry on a conversation like a real human. Why had I not continued with the next obvious question, "Oh! What do you do?" But my opportunity was gone and so were my secret hopes of learning more about what a real lesbian was like.

I could understand her lack of interest in friendship. What about me would have been intriguing to her? She was bronzed from the sun and walked with a swagger. She worshipped weed and Jesus. Riding her Harley in her free time was her happy place. My strongly hetero self smelled of the buttoned-up world of accounting and New England education. I bought sensible clothing that allowed me to blend in like grandma's wallpaper and dyed my shoulder-length hair blond. My singular act of rebellion, driving a black Mustang with racing stripes, was tempered with the fact that I followed all traffic laws and listened to Kelly Clarkson on the radio.

For months, Amy seemed to avoid my existence, instead hanging with a small girl gang that liked to gossip and chill out. I hung with the even smaller crowd that liked to crack open textbooks at lunch and review muscle attachment points. But there was one thing that drew us together. We both showed a mutual talent as massage therapists: I was a hard worker who studied, and she just seemed to be a natural. We realized that we liked being paired together during hands-on practice. I performed therapeutic techniques on her, she practiced the same on me, and we both felt better at the end of the day. There was a confidence to our touch when we worked. We both liked being in each other's energy. Eventually, there also seemed to be a social ease between us too. I'd say funny things that made her laugh. She'd say shockingly inappropriate things that made me gasp, which made her laugh even more.

While I attended massage school by day, I had picked up a part-time corporate job in the evening to help pay the bills. As soon as class finished, I would whirl into the bathroom like Superman, change from my massage outfit into my Clark Kent-ish dress pants and button-down shirt, and jet out of the school. My teachers chided me for throwing on pointy-toed heels that made me three inches taller and had me walking like a baby giraffe across the slippery school floor. But holding on to that way of dress allowed me to hold on to my corporate identity and not feel like I had thrown away everything I had worked for in college. It allowed me to keep a foot in both worlds: the land of auras, chimes, and vegan organic massage cream, and the land of cubicles, acronyms, and artificially flavored K-Cups.

It hit me harder than I would have ever imagined when my boss informed me that my department was being eliminated and I would receive two weeks of pay. Perhaps scarier than the loss of income was the loss of identity. I was now plunged fully into massage therapy. This was my first time not being corporate. My high heels could collect dust.

While I moped around like Princess Grumblepants, complaining to my classmates with words like *downsize* and *severance,* Amy told me in her most loving of ways to quit bitching. She had found an activity for my newly available free time. "Tomorrow, pack your swimsuit. We're going to the beach." This seemed wholly irresponsible of me to spend a Wednesday afternoon basking in the sun on the toasty Florida sand instead of sitting in a gray cubicle, pounding away at a keyboard for a paycheck. But she commanded and I found myself powerless to say no. Her blue-light glow was too strong for my mosquito brain to question.

The next day I was filled with excitement and nervous energy for our new afternoon plan. For me this was a bold move—taking time to not do anything, just be.

It felt foreign, as I had become accustomed to filling my minutes with busywork and meaningless distractions. Staying busy kept me in my head and out of my body. I had the feeling that a lot of people went through life that way too. Disembodied heads, filling their agendas and bank accounts while ignoring the emptiness inside them. But back to the beach. . . .

As class let out, we tossed on our two-piece bathing suits and hopped into our vehicles. I raced in my Mustang to keep up with her black pickup truck as she precariously swerved through traffic. She hadn't told me where we were going, just to follow. I did. My brain felt disengaged on this new adventure, and I smiled the whole drive. Adventure. Freedom. Perhaps even a bit of rebellion. There was no plan. Just her, me, and some undisclosed place with sand.

We pulled up to a little beach on an inlet of the Gulf of Mexico, in the retro town of Gulfport. Small gift shops and restaurants dotted the quiet main street. A few rainbow flags adorned the windows. We parked at the nearly empty beach and strolled close to the edge of the smooth water. I placed a blanket on the sand for both of us to lie on. Amy produced a lunch box with two peanut butter and blueberry jelly sandwiches, two bags of Sun Chips, and two Smirnoff Ices. This began our Wednesday afternoon ritual at one of the area's gay-friendly beaches. Until that moment, I didn't realize gay-friendly beaches were a thing.

Amy and I would alternate on bringing lunch each Wednesday, though it was always the same food that we packed. Chris questioned me as to why we suddenly had a stash of Smirnoff Ice in our fridge. I told him I had developed a taste for them. He tried to mask a look of disgust at my new habit and never brought up the subject again. I never hid the fact that Amy and I were having beach days, but I never felt compelled to share more than what he asked me.

On those sun-soaked days, where the weather was always perfect, we'd lie side by side on the nearly empty beach, tanning our bikini-clad skin and talking endlessly. She shared the challenges of her past and what it meant to grow up as a gay person in the Bible Belt state of Georgia. My heart broke for her several times over during her stories of hardship, violence, and rejection. I drank up each of her words like a thirsty sponge. I began to understand her hard exterior. She had been a target more than a few times, deflecting hurtful words and fists and creating a callous of toughness. But in those moments of vulnerability at the beach, I felt like I could also see her soul, which looked like a small, glowing gold ball in the center of a lot of darkness. It was soft and sad, but it was also good and wanted to be loved. I couldn't recall ever feeling like I had seen someone's soul before, but with her I didn't question it. I never told her what I saw. I was just grateful to be her safe space.

I loved those days together and the newness they brought to me. I was not used to having closeness with a friend, one who felt comfortable enough to confide in me, even if I was limited in what I confided in her. I wasn't used to taking time to just rest and couldn't remember the last time I had gone to the beach just for fun. I didn't really know what it meant to be gay and how queer people were treated. A subject that was always taboo in my world, I could suddenly learn about it even if I didn't know the questions to ask. She filled in the details. I just listened.

On those beach days, I felt alive. For a moment, I wondered if I could be having feelings for Amy. I found myself wanting people to see us together. I imagined them wondering to themselves if we were a couple. I pretended that they were cool with it and would tell us things, like what a cute pair we were. I daydreamed about what it might be like if people thought I was gay, even though I knew I wasn't. But what if they thought I was, and what if that was okay with them?

I stopped that wondering, realizing that my daydreams were crossing a line that a married woman should not cross. I changed the story. I reassured myself that this is what close female friendship felt like. And because I had not made many close female friendships in my teen and adult years, I convinced myself that what I felt for Amy was what friendship was supposed to be. Our closeness was the closeness of true friends. I was straight. She had no interest in me. We were only ever going to be friends.

Maybe.

My chest hurt on our last day of massage class before graduation. I wouldn't let myself think about the fact that it meant not seeing Amy every day and our beach trips would soon be a thing of the past. I cried alone in my car. I had an abysmal track record of keeping up with friendships for the long haul. I wanted to believe that I could be different with her and that our friendship could survive a little distance and days apart, but deep down I was scared. I worried that the feeling of being alive and wild would be extinguished if she wasn't there as my fuel. I didn't want to go back to the person I once was: the one who worked in a cubicle and tossed around corporate terminology, the one who feared confrontation and making anyone unhappy, the one who did exactly as she was told so everything would be perfect. I wanted to be brave and unapologetic, like Amy.

And so, after graduation, I vowed to make a change. I kept our friendship connection, going out of my way to drive the 40 minutes to her side of town to watch her softball games or have lunch with her on her work break. Sometimes, our relationship felt one-sided, but my brain never stayed upset for long. Like a mosquito to the blue light, I was irresistibly drawn to her.

THE LESBIAN EXPERIMENT

Chris was in Las Vegas for a bachelor party. As I sat home alone, watching reruns of *Supermarket Sweep*, my phone lit up with the blue glow of a text. It was Amy. My mind did a mini–happy dance just knowing she was reaching out to me. The happy dance turned into a full-on mental flash mob of excitement when I read on.

"Do you want to go out with us tonight?"

My stomach did backflips and I waited for more details.

"We're going to Georgie's Alibi. It's a gay bar . . . obviously."

Had it been any other person and any other place, the introvert in me would have cowered in fear at the thought of socializing with a new crowd. But tonight my brain had already slapped on some lipstick and was sitting in the car just waiting to make the drive.

"Of course!" I responded, sounding overly eager. Of course I would hang out with her and her girlfriend. Of course I would go to a gay bar. Of course I wanted to do these things.

Part of me wondered if I was making the right choice, but I was an expert at mental gymnastics at that point and convinced myself it was a completely reasonable thing to do. As a married heterosexual woman, a gay bar made perfect sense. There would be no chance that I would be picked up by men, that is unless they were kindly carrying me closer to the stage to watch the drag show. And Amy was there with her girlfriend, which was great since there never was and never would be anything going on between us anyway.

I turned my thoughts to Las Vegas. Chris was probably in far more precarious positions at that moment, surrounded by strippers and bartenders offering to lighten his wallet. It was fine. We could handle ourselves. I continued this self-assuring conversation in my mind for the next hour as I got ready.

Deciding what to wear became one of the hardest parts of my evening. Amy had a decidedly masculine style. It dawned on me that I had never thought about what section of the department store she bought her clothes from, or if she even shopped at department stores. Where did butch women shop? The mainstream fashion market and retail space certainly didn't seem to acknowledge the existence of females with masculine style. I couldn't imagine that her petite size was easy to come by in the men's department. Amy's girlfriend, by contrast, was described to me as a "lipstick lesbian." That definition made zero sense to me at the time because she never wore lipstick. She did have long blond hair, wore tight jeans, and would occasionally wear a shoe with a modest, chunky heel. She was decidedly more feminine, but with an edge to her. Feminine but different. Perhaps this was the meaning of *je ne sais quoi,* that energetic quality that you just can't quite pinpoint.

I couldn't figure out where I fit into this equation. My goal for the night was to not stand out like an obvious hetero thumb, but also to not lose myself trying to blend in. I opted for a black cashmere halter top that I rarely had the guts to wear. But it made me feel attractive and highlighted my back, shoulders, and arms, all of which had become nicely toned with my massage therapy work. I paired it with some skinny jeans and, after much deliberation, tossed on my strappy black high heels. I've always loved wearing heels. Heels felt like ownership and confidence, both of which I lacked in that moment.

I always felt a mix of nervous excitement when I was with Amy, but this new foray into the world of gay bars took that energy to a new level of internal anxiety. When I arrived at her house, Amy did a once-over glance of my outfit and murmured an "okay" with a complete deadpan look. I wasn't sure if I had passed the test.

The doorbell rang and in strutted Amy's friend, a woman with vibrant golden hair like an untamed lion's mane. She had the biggest green eyes with the longest, most mascaraed eyelashes I had ever seen. I feared every time she blinked that the top and bottom lashes would get stuck together like Velcro.

There was also a sweetness in her eyes that seemed to be in opposition to the "I can take care of myself" air that surrounded her. My high heels, which put me a good foot above her in height, were not enough. Something about her made me nervous, like she could see right through me. I wondered if Amy sensed it. She didn't help to make the situation better.

"This is my 'straight' friend, Jill," Amy said, making air quotes with her fingers to emphasize the *straight*. Panic. My quickly deflating balloon of confidence was nearly out of air. My mind raced with equally opposite thoughts of, *Does Amy really think I could be gay? How dare she! I'm a married woman . . . going to a gay bar . . . with a bunch of lesbians . . . wearing an outfit that I've never worn out with my straight friends.*

What was I?

My mind reassured me that I was straight and that this would just be a great night full of dancing, drag queens, and self-doubt.

When we arrived, my insides started to feel like someone had just dropped a Mentos into a bottle of Coke and quickly put the cap back on. All the bubbles welled up and I did my best not to explode my guts like a mile-high geyser on the dance floor. *Cool it, Jill!*, I told myself. *Be like a human. Be normal. Try it for once.*

The bar was fun. I won't go into details because it was a bar. Picture any dark, hazy bar. It was that. We ordered a round of Smirnoffs and set out on the dance floor. There are a few odd moments that remained sharply embedded in my brain from that night:

(1) Being painfully self-aware as I overwatched Amy and her girlfriend dance together. I was filled with happiness that this was a real thing that two women could do, jealousy that I wasn't doing the same, and fear that this was not actually allowed and somebody would come along and make them stop.

(2) Having my drink bottle clinked in "cheers" by the butchiest butch in the place and being curious as to whether it was because I fit in or because I stood out in a painfully obvious way.

(3) Going to the bathroom and wondering if couples ever came in together to make out . . . since they could. You could be in the same restroom as your significant other. It was an odd revelation. I know. And the reality was that in this gay bar they were safe to make out anywhere, so why resign themselves to the crowded, unsanitary bathroom? Clearly, I was already in an odd state of mind. My curiosity about what could go on in the women's bathroom cycled through my mind for most of the night. That is, until Amy's friend took my hand.

Her untamed curls (or perhaps it was her eyelashes) whipped around as she grabbed my wrist and pulled me firmly against her petite body. Lightning went through me as I felt her strength. Then she whispered into my ear, "My ex is over there. Pretend you're my girlfriend."

Hop back to my metaphor of Mentos in Coke. Imagine the pressure inside that bottle just before the cap shoots off. All the bubbles, fighting toward the surface and pushing outward in every direction. That was my insides. I wasn't attracted to this woman in that sense, but the thought of getting to pretend I was a lesbian felt both terrifying and thrilling. I prayed that I wouldn't explode.

Instead, I froze. My scrawny arm was awkwardly posed across her shoulder as if I were a plastic doll with minimally mobile joints. I hoped that somehow my stiffness wouldn't be noticed. I gave myself a pep talk that was rooted in advice of Tyra Banks from her show *America's Next Top Model.* I was going to have to try and communicate with my eyes, since I already knew words would be failing me. I tried to channel my best "this is *my* girlfriend" stare, gazing with equal parts flirt and possessiveness.

As she began to chat with her ex, I realized that I didn't know what to do with my other hand. Should I have it on some part of her? On my waist to puff me up like a cocky peafowl? I also didn't know how to turn my body. Toward her? Toward the ex? Most importantly, I didn't have the faintest clue how to act like I was in a relationship with this person in any way whatsoever.

One obnoxious brain cell screamed at me the friendly reminder that I was married to a man. As the two women talked, their conversation with each other became a buzz of static in my ears, as I was now completely wrapped up in my own mind. Then the ex walked away. *Yes!* I had done it. Operation Lez Pretend completed! I felt my innards unclench.

She turned toward me. I smiled back like a happy puppy waiting for praise. Her brilliant emerald eyes turned and gazed deep into mine as she said, "You're terrible at this." Lesbian experiment over.

SAINT JOHN

Maybe it's because I'm a perfectionist. Perhaps it's because I'm an Aries. But when I do something, I do it to the nth degree.

"Oh, you want to start running for fun? I think I'll sign up for a little half-marathon to really challenge myself!"

"You're bringing brownies to the girls' night out? That's nice. Let me just research the most nutritionally dense, raw, vegan cashew dream cake I can whip up in a mere seventy-two hours!"

"Washing your hands? Let me dazzle you with the eco-friendliest way to dry them using only half a paper towel and inertia!"

Yeah, you can say it. I annoy the fuck out of myself sometimes too.

At this point, I decided to throw myself back into my marriage. My experience at the gay bar had only proven to me how straight I was. Even if I *wanted* to be gay, which

I didn't, I wasn't good at it and I didn't want to be "not good" at anything. My life drifted further from those lazy beach days and back into work mode and routine. The perfectionist within me had climbed back onto her throne. I was laser-focused on one goal—it was time to perfect being a wife to Chris and a daughter to my mom.

Chris and I talked about starting a family. The conversation went something like this, "Do you think now would be a good time to try having a baby?" Approximately 27 hours to two weeks later: "Oh look! I'm pregnant!" I added "fertilizing embryo in my uterus" to the skills section of my résumé and applauded our efficiency.

My pregnancy was the textbook best-case scenario with every checkup from our midwife. Aside from needing an iron supplement, my vitals were good and so were Baby Sophie's. Sophie grew the correct amount with each appointment, and as I studied books and videos on labor, I was sure my labor experience would be textbook as well. I did what I always do in every life scenario and prepared and planned as much as I thought possible.

However, at the time there was only one outcome I saw in my mind: I would go into labor on Christmas Eve, Sophie's due date. I would have a storybook-worthy water birth in my home. And within a few short hours of managing my contractions effectively through movement, soaking, and chanting "om," I would be holding the most beautiful baby child in my arms and would be filled with a love like no other, just in time for Santa Claus to pop down the chimney and gift me a toaster oven.

I don't mean to shock you, but none of that happened.

Sophie was two weeks late and nearing the point where I would potentially have to be induced in the hospital. I wanted my home birth. It was my plan. When my contractions started around midnight, the pain was so intense that I convinced myself that I must be deep in the throes of labor. My body ached so badly with each contraction that I figured I must be close to fully dilated and Sophie's birth would be imminent. It hurt, but I was keeping it together and doing fine.

I called Chris, who was out with a friend who was visiting town. The text message said something to the extent of, "Hey, you might want to close out your tab now. Baby." I called my midwife, who drove over in her mobile office RV. She walked into the house, woolen knit cap on her head and eyes still full of sleep. I greeted her with an excited smile. It was time to pop out a baby!

She gave me a half-smile, while looking only slightly annoyed that I had woken her up in the middle of her sleep. "You are *way* too happy to be in active labor right now," she said, deflating my emotional balloon that had banked on the contraction pain being over soon. I asked her to check me so that at least I could plan how much longer this discomfort might go on for. I was a whopping one centimeter dilated . . . maybe. Barely one! I thought I was finishing a marathon race and it was like she had told me that the first water station was still three miles away. This was going to be a long day.

She went upstairs in my house and went to bed. I read the motivational quotes that I had typed and hung around my bedroom walls, cursing every single one as hippy-dippy bullshit. These motivational quotes were clearly not written by anyone who had ever experienced the sheer pain of unmedicated labor. Focus on your breathing? Turn within? I'll show you where you can shove your self-awareness! (Okay, so perhaps I should have included a doula or some hypnobirthing in my birth planning to chill my rage-labor feelings.)

After 23 hours of contractions, an unusable birthing tub due to our old house not being able to produce enough hot water, stitches from tearing during labor, and a solid amount of blood loss, I was lying in bed with my beautiful and perfectly healthy new baby girl in my arms. And I felt nothing except exhaustion. I tried breastfeeding and marveled at the cascade of baby vomit that she would produce shortly after eating. She never seemed satisfied. I was failing as a mom already.

Perhaps the hardest thing for me about labor and becoming a mother was that it taught me that, despite my best efforts at control, I wasn't in control. And the more years that passed in life, the more I felt that control slipping away. Gone were the rewards for completing homework or acing a test. Nobody gave me a trophy for the amount of money I saved on my groceries. There was no perfect attendance award for showing up to work every day.

I was now realizing that those types of extrinsic rewards had propped me up for so long but didn't leave me feeling full. In fact, now I didn't seem to know how to feel good if someone wasn't telling me how good I was doing. Sometimes I looked at my life, perfect in every way possible, and wondered, *Is this* it*? Is* this *what living is supposed to feel like?* I felt guilty about not being content with everything I had, but I was aching for that feeling of being alive. And now, here I was, having brought a new life into this world and feeling so far from being alive myself.

My mind started to spiral as I realized I was both living the American dream and still feeling unsatisfied. I had achieved what so many in this world dream of having, and yet I didn't feel any better, or happier, or more satisfied. And if this wasn't it, what level would I have to achieve to get that satisfaction? How much did I get to ask for? How much did I deserve? And did I even deserve to feel this way, since so many others in the world live with far less? There were people in my own community who begged for money and food. Here I was, begging for something to fill the empty space that money and food couldn't fill. I felt like an asshole for wanting an intangible thing. I wanted happiness. Why didn't I have it? My life was perfect. I was fine.

I needed help, but I wasn't sure where to even begin. I was bedridden after labor and sensed a long road of recovery ahead of me. I felt physically wrecked, but the emotional pain was what really hurt. I decided to set up a home visit with a CST practitioner named Dawn. I knew craniosacral therapy might be able to address both the physical and the emotional pieces. I had met Dawn, with her long salt-and-pepper-colored hair and wisdom-filled skin, during my time at the massage school. While my focus on massage had been on deep tissue and anything that fit the "no pain, no gain" theory, she introduced me to the world of light touch and energy work. And her work involved going to the Bahamas each year for dolphin-assisted therapy. This woman had serious street cred as a cool therapist.

CST is a useful modality in that it is done with the client fully dressed and has very few contraindications or age restrictions. Dawn explained that the real power in craniosacral therapy was that it not only addressed the physical body but could also facilitate the release of emotional and energetic traumas as well. "The issues are in the tissues," she would say, alluding to the fact that our brain cells were not the only ones that store memories. I didn't know that I believed her. I didn't understand how that could be the truth, that she could somehow feel restrictions in my body caused by memories or emotions. But I did recognize that birth was a traumatic experience for the birther and the baby, regardless of the ease and outcome, and I was willing to give craniosacral therapy a try so that my child and I could start our journey together on the most optimal path.

Sophie's session was fascinating to watch. Dawn cradled all eight pounds of pudgy baby in her arms as Sophie contorted her newborn body, twisting and turning like a baby reptile emerging from an egg. We soon realized that she was re-creating the birthing position that she was in down the birth canal, complete with her clenched fist pushing at her jaw like a fighter taking an uppercut. She held a brief moment of tension in that position and then she flopped her body loosely, arms and legs fully extended. Sophie smiled as the craniosacral practitioner passed her back to me. This wasn't the smile of a baby passing gas. This was the smile of relief.

I was in awe of what I had just witnessed and wouldn't have believed it myself had I not seen it happen right there in front of me. I hoped to experience the same level of relief and renewal during my own session. Dawn reminded me that in craniosacral therapy, the client's body is the guide and the practitioner just holds the space for healing to occur. She couldn't make anything happen. She couldn't control what my body wanted to release, nor what it wanted to hold on to. I, or more specifically, my body was in control of the session.

She equated craniosacral therapy to seeing a client sitting in the mud at the bottom of a hole. Her job was not to find me a ladder or a rope to climb out. Her job wasn't to climb into the hole and give me a boost to get out of the hole. Her role as practitioner was to sit with me in the mud so that I didn't have to be alone until I could figure my own way out. Deep, self-led healing . . . that my inner perfectionist snarked at because, obviously, I didn't need healing. I was fine.

It only took what felt like a few minutes for me to fall asleep hard, a result of my sympathetic nervous system, in nearly constant fight-or-flight mode, being given permission to relax. That one-hour nap session on her therapy table felt like a full night of sleep to my body that had been pushed to its limits.

When I came to, I began to feel capable again. There was hope that I would be able to rejoin society sometime in the future and resume my level of productivity. I wish I could have just let myself rest, but I didn't understand the value of it back then. Resting, pausing, going inward—they're not a sign of weakness, they're a rebuilding of strength. Why could I acknowledge that rest was necessary for people and yet not allow myself the grace to go through it as well?

Dawn concluded the session by gently asking if I had heard of St. John's wort. She added, "It may help you."

"Okay," I nodded, like I knew what I was talking about. I was too embarrassed to ask what it was for, and I definitely didn't have the courage to question why she sensed that I might need some help. Maybe I was more scared of hearing the answer. I decided I would Google it later.

St. John's wort, according to the first result on Google, is "an herbal remedy that has been used for hundreds of years to treat mental health problems. Today it is mainly used as an over-the-counter remedy to treat mild and moderate depression." *I don't need that,* I told myself. I was fine.

STAGE TWO

CONFUSION

TEMPTATION AND TRIGGER POINTS

I wasn't fine.

I was hollow, seeking fullness. In my role as a new mom, I struggled desperately to connect with my baby girl in the way that so many other new parents seemed to be able to do with ease. I didn't understand why I felt like I was fumbling through motherhood, like someone had just handed me a baby wombat instead of a baby human. I yearned for those maternal instincts that were supposed to come naturally. Chris and I joked that he was the better mom, waking up at her every whimper during the night, while I slept like a snoring lumberjack. Joking about it helped me hide the fact that I was ashamed of how I was performing as a mother. I didn't know it was supposed to be hard.

My mom and I took Sophie for a walk around the neighborhood in her stroller. Looking down at her chubby pink face, I tearfully shared that I felt no more connected to her than if any other random baby on Earth were placed in that stroller. Even though I had birthed her, I sometimes felt like someday her real mom would show up at the door and I would watch them leave, as I thanked them for the babysitting experience and newly stretched out vagina. I loved Sophie as a human but struggled to understand what it meant to love her as my daughter. My mom assured me that this was probably from the exhaustion of labor and being a new parent. She seemed confident that our bond would grow with time. Nobody, including myself, ever brought up the words *postpartum depression*. Years later, many of my friends realized that they had gone through it too. Yet in the first weeks and months postbirth, none of us shared the negative feelings, hallucinations, or panic attacks that motherhood had gifted us. We were all supposed to be fine. Our babies came first now.

Inside me echoed a voice begging me to find that inner light again. I was desperate for it. Being a new mom allowed me many hours at home to tend to the baby and daydream. My thoughts would always wander back to those safe Sapphic shadows of my past. I would rock Sophie in my arms while replaying the details of my days at the beach with Amy, the visits to the gay bars, the softball games where Amy and her partner played in an all-lesbian league. These were the times when I felt different. I felt happier.

I wanted to seek comfort in the queer world. I hoped for any opportunity to hang out with Amy and my other LGBTQ+ friends. I had reached the point where I wanted to be as close to gay as possible, without actually being gay. I wanted the light I felt from the gay community, without the darkness from society that came from being a member of the gay community.

As I questioned my sanity as a mother, I questioned my identity as a heterosexual. Did other straight people find the same happiness around the gay community that I did? Was it just the glitter and rainbows? The sense of belonging to a chosen family and the opportunity to shoot a bubble gun on a Pride parade float? Or did I feel more at home with them because . . . perhaps . . . maybe . . . I might be one of them?

I felt like Ariel in Disney's *The Little Mermaid,* minus the curiosity with dinglehoppers. I was living the cushy, comfortable life of heteronormativity, while every free moment was preoccupied with thoughts of the queer world that I could only dabble in occasionally. As Ariel learned in the movie, at some point you have to choose one world or the other. You don't get land legs and underwater breathing abilities. I couldn't have a husband in real life and a wife in my dreams. I realized that if my energy continued to be directed toward the gay community, there would be a reckoning with my marriage. And although I felt like an inadequate mother, I couldn't give up my family life. We had just gotten started. There would be no making deals for a chance at the lesbian life with a drag queen named Ursula.

So, I did what any sane and rational person would do when faced with such a predicament. I suggested we move to a new country.

On a trip home from visiting Chris's family in the Dominican Republic, I proposed that we pick up our lives and move overseas with our one-year-old daughter to a foreign land to help the family run their business. Outwardly it made sense. Chris was frustrated in a stale corporate job. Sophie was at a prime age to become a bilingual baby. I could take my massage therapy skills anywhere. His family was elated to have their son and grandbaby nearby. We would be surrounded by mangoes, and rum, and beaches, and Roman Catholicism.

Privately, I knew it also made sense as well. As far as I was aware, the Dominican Republic had no visible gay community at that time thanks to its strong religious roots. There would be no more temptation for me. No more people or places to daydream about. No more invites from Amy to attend lesbian baby showers or Pride parties. I could just focus on my marriage and test how many espressos I could drink in a day before my heart felt like it might rupture. Life would be good. Our family would be okay. Moving to another country to escape gay life didn't seem like a drastic measure at the time, and I hoped things would work out.

Clearly, I didn't understand how these feelings worked.

Acclimating to life in the Dominican Republic was a good, new challenge to focus on. I settled into a polite and well-dressed circle of heterosexual females in the International Women's Club. We wore blouses and dress pants, cocktail dresses, and oversized sunglasses. Chris devoted his waking hours to proving his worth in the family business, while Sophie and I sat home staring at the clock, desperate for the end of the workday. There were only so many hours that we could distract ourselves with attempts to learn Spanish from watching episodes of *Los Wiggles* on TV.

After several months, I realized I needed to branch out and build my new identity as we tried to establish permanent roots. I started a mobile massage therapy practice, made easier by the fact that I had a driver to take me around town and schlep my massage table up four flights of stairs. My fledgling business turned out to be quite popular with the international inhabitants who sought therapeutic massage. I began to feel more in my element again. I loved the fulfillment that I got from performing therapeutic massage work and helping people overcome pain. The hollowness was still within me, but at least now I had the newness of everything else to keep me distracted.

Until there was Anja—the one who started as a client and then became a friend, inviting me to stay for a coffee, organic fruit, and imported chocolates after her appointments. She was a slender, olive-skinned European with a neatly trimmed, sleek, brown bob. My American sensibility was unaccustomed to and uncomfortable with how free she was in her own body. Anja would walk into the room completely naked without an ounce of embarrassment. I wondered how people could do that—just walk around naked and feel secure in their skin. I would quickly avert my body-ashamed gaze and ask her to cover herself between the top sheet and the fitted sheet.

She was an attractive woman, but I was not attracted to her. At least, that was the story I told myself. I just had an appreciation for and the ability to recognize beauty, like all humans did. Women could look at other women and think they were beautiful. Men could identify other men as being attractive. Besides, I no longer thought I was gay. I had proven my heterosexuality to myself by resisting and escaping the gay culture of Tampa Bay. I was now just a woman, married to a man, with a baby, living in a country where same-sex relationships would send you straight to the fiery pits of El Infierno. Gay was not okay. Hetero would be better-o.

Was she attracted to me? Also no, I told myself. She was also married to a man, with a child, living in a country where anything more than friendship would not have been well received. And her need for frequent nudity? I chalked up my discomfort and her complete comfort with the naked body to cultural differences.

I was a professional. My massages had been and were always therapeutic. No boundaries would ever be crossed. I was here to work on muscles, tendons, and ligaments. And she was just a person from a part of Europe who had been raised without puritanical shame. This was no big deal.

When she complained of low back and hip pain, I dug my knuckles into the edge of her sacrum, waiting for the muscle tissue to soften around her tailbone so that I could begin more focused trigger point work. She was muscular like a ballet dancer, long and lean from her regular routine of Pilates and yoga. As the bones of my hands sunk deeper into her tissue, she spoke through the face cradle.

"I wish you could be inside of me."

I could hear my heart begin to beat in my ears and throb intensely all over my body. There was a cataclysmic shift in my energy, with feelings of both fear and fire. I held my breath and my exterior became rigid, as if freezing my limbs would contain what was happening inside. This was sheer panic. My mind replayed her words on a loop: *I wish you could be inside of me. I wish you could be inside of me.* I never knew that hearing those words out loud could have the ability to unravel me in the way that it did.

She caught me off guard and was now proving how foolish my plan of moving overseas to try and change myself really was. I didn't know what she meant by that statement, but I also no longer cared. I realized, as soon as those words had an effect on me, that I was failing at straightening myself out. Shame crept in as I waited for her to say more, not knowing which direction I wanted the meaning of her words to take. Could this just be a therapeutic request that was lost in translation? Could another woman really want me in that way?

I did a quick grounding exercise to regain my composure and kept working in silence, moving to her calf muscles to scan for trigger points and signal that this would be just a regular massage and nothing more. My mind couldn't think of a single thing to say. (Damn you, Ursula, you took my voice!) I felt embarrassed and sad. My appointments and friendship with her had been one of the bright points during my difficult times overseas. My reaction to her told me I would no longer be able to continue this therapeutic relationship. There were feelings there. She stayed silent too.

I didn't see her again. I realized that, despite my best efforts, my external environment couldn't change the person I was starting to figure out inside of me. These feelings of attraction to women weren't going away, no matter what corner of the planet I ran to. I wasn't sure what to do anymore. My marriage was at risk.

Nothing hurts the heart like a slow break.

WATERFALLS AND WIVES

You may or may not have picked up by now that drastic measures are a "thing" with me. When the going gets tough, I fight harder, go bigger, do the unimaginable to make things happen. So, as I watched another crack form in my marriage, I figured I would fix it with some relationship caulk—and have another baby.

It wasn't quite that cavalier or crass. Remember here, you're dealing with an experienced perfectionist who over-analyzes and self-critiques to an unhealthy measure. No decision is taken lightly. However, at that point I began to be filled with a real fear that I would not be able to carry out my marriage "till death do us part" if something didn't change. Rather than focus my energy on erasing gay thoughts from my mind, I redirected myself more deeply into something that with time I had come to love and excel at—being a mother. And if one baby was a ton of work, two babies would surely keep my mind on my family and push me further from those chances of experiencing what life might be like if I was part of the LGBTQ+ community.

Although we were still living in the Dominican Republic when I got pregnant, my local obstetrician advised me to give birth in the U.S. if I had the option. I wanted an unmedicated vaginal delivery, and that just wasn't commonplace at her hospital. Every few months, I began flying back to Florida to meet with my midwife at a beautiful birthing center in Sarasota called Rosemary Court. It was heavenly to me. Rosemary Court, a collection of small cottages on one property, had an energy to it like an adult granola Disneyland. One cottage was the birthing center, another a yoga studio, another a craniosacral therapy center. I have never felt more safe and held in a space. If there was a place that could simulate the protective growth environment of a uterus, Rosemary Court was it. Uteri on Earth!

My midwife team was skilled, soft, and gentle. Fear around birthing was still deep within me. I didn't know if I could endure the physical damage and postpartum depression that accompanied Sophie's birth. They suggested I try craniosacral therapy at the cottage within their community. They spoke of Agnieszka, the CST practitioner from Poland, like she was a magical creature from a magical land. And she was. If my craniosacral practitioner from Sophie's birth had been a college-level athlete, Agnieszka would have ranked like an Olympic medalist.

I began to see her for an appointment every time I was back in the United States. She intuitively worked around my ever-growing body, and I marveled at how Oliver, from my womb, seemed to communicate with her whenever she was near. The two of them developed a bond, separated only by the thin wall of abdominal tissue in their way. I felt like an audience member at an enthralling performance between a practitioner and a baby. When Agnieszka asked me if I'd be willing to receive CST while I was in labor, I jumped at the opportunity. She was excited to meet Oliver, and I was excited for anything that might make labor less laborious.

Oliver's birth was life-changing. It was one of those pivot points when you start as one person and end as another. I shed an old way of being and was stepping into a new phase. The word *midwife* means "woman who is 'with,'" and here I was surrounded by a team of caring women where my voice felt heard. They were on my side. They supported me and were skillful at including Chris in the labor circle as an important participant but not the decision-maker. We operated as one unit, but I was fully in control and taking the lead.

It was the first time in recent history I could recall that I acted in a way that I wanted to act, not in the way I thought I should be acting. It made me think of how many times in sex I had moaned or arched my body in a certain way because that was how I thought women were supposed to respond. I wondered how I would respond during sex if I could have just let go like I was now during labor. What if I wasn't there to perform for another? What if I was just there for me?

In this labor, if I wanted something, I asked for it. If I wanted to growl or flap my lips like a horse, I did. If I wanted to walk around naked, unrestricted by fabric, I did so without an ounce of shame. My previously prudish self, who was completely uncomfortable with nudity, was now like my confident European massage client. I was proud of my body and what it was doing, and I didn't feel shamed into covering it up for someone else's comfort. I wasn't sure how or why craniosacral therapy was bringing my inner knowing outward, but I felt the most aware of who I was and what I wanted in those 19 hours of exertion.

All of this—being in my body, staying present, giving myself and Oliver what we needed while we labored—I credit to the CST. It had taken me out of my mind and into my heart space. I felt part human, part animal, but completely full. There was no space for shame. Fear was gone. This was my experience, and I could steer it in the direction I wanted it to go. I knew CST was effective after my first birth experience with Sophie, but Oliver's birth showed me that it could take me to a whole new level of stepping into my true self. It created a bridge between the person I had tried to be in my first labor and who I actually was in my second labor. This was powerful knowledge that a deeper Jill existed, and CST could bring me closer to her.

This Jill knew her place was back in the U.S. permanently. I no longer needed to run from myself. Chris agreed that it was the right move for our family and his career to return to Florida. Much to my mom's elation, we were Tampa residents once again. My community was there, and I now tasked myself with figuring out how to have the best of both worlds—a closeness to the queer culture that lit me up inside while serving my family as the best possible wife and mother. It would take balance and boundaries, but it was the only way for me to have it all. "Till death" actually seemed more doable.

BLACK HOLES

Isn't it adorable how our bodies can bury memories away deep in our cells, sealing them off like sweet little doom packages that could explode with the most unsuspecting trigger? Like the time I was watching the movie *The Prom*, about a teenager who wants to attend prom with her girlfriend and faces resistance from the school board. I burst into tears when the head of the school board, Mrs. Greene (played by Kerry Washington), shared with her daughter (who she didn't realize was gay) that she would never want a gay child because life would just be harder for them. The tears flowed from my eyeholes as I recalled hearing the same from my own mom during my teenage years. It was a fleeting comment made only one time in my entire life to which my mind said, *Oh, let's just hold on to that difficult memory and put a bow on it to unwrap later!*

"I wouldn't want a gay child" should not have stuck with me in my teens if I had no idea I was possibly gay then. It showed me that, regardless of how straight I thought I was, my body knew better and identified that line as being something significant. My mom hadn't said it to be hurtful or outwardly homophobic. I recall in the same conversation her sharing that the reason she wouldn't want a gay child was because it added more obstacles and hardships to life. Now as a mother myself, I understood the desire to keep suffering out of my children's lives. Through more experience with craniosacral therapy, though, I realized how many well-intentioned words I had received in my past that actually caused suffering. Parenting sometimes feels like a no-win game. Sometimes, in an effort to prevent or avoid pain, we cause more of it.

After Oliver's incredibly powerful birth experience with craniosacral therapy, I dove headfirst into studying the work myself so that I could begin to help others experience the same healing. I took a four-day intensive course to learn how to perceive and address physical, emotional, and energetic blockages with just five grams of pressure in my hands as they sandwiched various parts of my clients' bodies. I joined a local craniosacral therapy study group of experienced practitioners that felt more like a meeting of superheroes with powerful intuitive abilities. And I continued to receive the work myself with various practitioners, as each one brought out different blocks in my own personal healing.

One session found me on the table of a particularly perceptive healer. I marveled during the session at how quickly her hands moved from one area to the next on my body, and how quickly my intuition could figure out what the block was related to and release it through talking, or tears, or whatever other emotion arose. She was an elderly woman who had been treating people using craniosacral therapy for nearly 30 years, just about the amount of time I had been on Earth. This session was like therapy at warp speed. My body was hungry for healing that day.

We were nearing the end of a session that had its fair share of mini breakthroughs about small stressors in my life. I was feeling good, and I figured we'd be wrapping up shortly with some nice grounding energy. Then I would pay her and be on my way to mop floors and prepare peanut butter and jelly sandwiches for my small humans.

But before we finished, there was one more area she was called to work on. Her hands gently cupped over my liver area, with one of her hands on my abdomen and one hand gently touching my back. I suddenly got a vision so strong it was like a TV had just been switched on in my mind. I saw brown, desolate ground and, off in the distance a bit, was a black hole in the soil. I edged closer to the hole, realizing it was a bottomless pit. I felt overcome by a knowing that if I fell into that deep cavern, it would have me falling through darkness for eternity. I backed away, but now I saw myself as a child standing at the edge of that hole, staring down into it. I saw fear in my younger self. She just gazed down, unmoving. Fear started to permeate my own adult cells on the table and the CST practitioner felt it.

"What's here?" she asked. I looked at the younger version of me standing at the edge of darkness, wondering what was there and why it was making me feel so awful. To you, reader, the answer is probably painfully obvious. But to me, in that moment I struggled to make sense of what in my life could cause this level of terror within me. What could be important enough that it would bore a hole through me and cause this level of worry? Work? Family? Finances? I checked off the most obvious (and superficial) boxes, eventually realizing that I was dancing around the truth.

I knew what that black hole was. I prayed that I could be anywhere in the world besides on that therapy table, standing at the edge of my greatest fear. It was almost unbearable. My rational mind fought to regain control of the situation. I told myself we were *not* going there and tightened my lips as if somehow closing my mouth could stop the truth from being real. The infinite darkness of the hole was just inches from my childhood feet. I didn't move a muscle for fear of falling in.

You don't have to say anything, Jill. She doesn't have to know. This doesn't have to be your truth, I told myself like some negotiator talking to a terrorist who had taken over my innards. I didn't know if I was ready for it.

The practitioner may have felt my internal struggle. "This goes back to about third grade," she added serenely with a gentle smile on her face. She didn't seem remotely bothered by the chaos I was now feeling inside. But rather than calm me, her words and her specific knowledge sent me deeper into worry.

She knows! How does she know?! My body screamed. There could be no hiding it now. I hadn't even said my truth and yet somehow part of it was already out there. An image of the first girl I had ever had a crush on popped into my mind's TV. The practitioner was right. It was absolutely third grade. The girl and I belonged to the same dance performance group. Her name was also Jill, and I remember thinking at the time that she was the most beautiful person I had ever seen. I felt drawn to her and completely, utterly shy about getting anywhere near her presence. I was around eight years old, though, and I didn't understand what I was feeling toward her or why.

The practitioner somehow was watching my mind's TV set too. There was nothing left to hide.

"I know what it is," I mumbled, as my mind questioned my sanity for initiating this conversation with a woman who could have very well been my grandmother. Discussing my sexuality didn't feel at all polite or appropriate, and I wished we were discussing sewing patterns or garden flowers instead. Her hands hovered patiently over the black hole on my torso while my words finally pushed their way past my lips.

"It's related to my attraction," I continued. This was a testing of the waters to see if a verbal reveal would be okay. She didn't flinch and her kind expression never changed. Perhaps this would be okay, I reassured myself as I attempted to breathe. I was convinced that somehow, she already knew exactly what I was going to say, so my reveal shouldn't be such a big deal.

This was it. Time to put the truth out there into the world for the first time ever.

"I'm . . ." I whispered, entering the point of no return. "I'm . . . bisexual."

In my mind's eye, I watched the black hole gape open through my back body at those words. Jet black tar cascaded out of me, rapidly pooling on the floor and spilling into each corner of the room. I worried about it ruining her carpet and then remembered that this darkness flowing from me wasn't real, in the earthly physical sense, that is. As the emotional darkness seemed to exit my body, tears flowed from my eyes and pooled in my ears. The release was huge. Year and years of shame, fear, doubt, and loathing were starting to leave. Damn, it felt good. What relief!

That relief was only partial, though. As soon as *bisexual* reached the light of day, I knew it wasn't the truth. It was like a half-truth. It was my safe truth that would allow me to keep one foot in the land of heterosexuality, while acknowledging my attraction to women. It was the label that would allow me to validate why I was in a relationship with Chris, while still allowing myself permission to be attracted to the same gender.

Bisexuality is a completely valid identity for many in the LGBTQ+. Earlier in my life, when I didn't have the language or frame of reference for my feelings, my attraction may have been to men and women. Bisexuality could have been my truth . . . at some point. But sexuality is also fluid, and now I recognized that identifying as bisexual to the practitioner didn't feel like my honest truth. It was truth lite—all the internal homosexual guilt, but with all the outward hetero benefits. I wondered if she'd be able to pick up on my lack of truth too. If she could sense it, would she think the lie was my attraction to men or my attraction to women? I hoped she would just accept what I said.

"Around third grade is the first time I remember being attracted to a girl," I continued. "We used to dance together and . . ."

"You wanted to dance like her," she chimed in, with more of a statement than a question.

Oof. No. This was unusual. I knew from my craniosacral training that we were not supposed to fill in the blanks for our clients when they spoke. Their truth was their reality, regardless of what we thought of it or any opinions we had about it. The space was no longer feeling safe. I started to close up.

No! I said to myself, no longer wishing to verbalize my thoughts aloud. I continued the conversation in my mind.

I wanted to feel her arms wrap around me. I wanted to look into her green eyes and feel her soft, bronze skin and know what it was like to be that close to her.

She paused, waiting for me to fill in the silence, but I couldn't carry on this conversation anymore. Not honestly, anyway. I had shifted out of my body's open emotions and completely back into my protective, rational mind. *Save me, self!* I just nodded my head and affirmed her statement. I had not come in today prepared to speak my truth, and the subtle cue that what I said was not okay left me feeling unable to speak. She continued the conversation, telling me how this girl was probably a really good dancer and it's not surprising that I wanted to emulate her. That was a completely normal feeling, she assured me.

The black tar was no longer pouring out of me. However, my initial feelings of pride for facing my fear were nearly gone. Shame was taking over and filling in the empty spaces inside of me where love should have gone. She had confirmed that who I was, was not okay. I had clearly made her feel uncomfortable. I regretted my decision to come out. I was no longer perfect in her eyes.

"Sometimes we feel confused toward our female friends," she finished. I shrank deeper into myself. I knew she was incorrect. I was not confused. In fact, sharing my truth on her table made me feel the least confused I had ever been. It was becoming clear to me what I wanted back then as a child and why those feelings only continued to grow as I got older. I felt weakened by her filling in the blanks of my story, though.

I sat up from the table, using half a box of tissues to wipe the tears and snot from my blotchy red face. My people-pleasing instincts wondered how I could make this situation better for her. Perhaps I could pay her more. Perhaps I could somehow mind-erase her and we could pretend like what I said to her never actually happened. It didn't matter that for that brief moment on the table, when I shared that I was not straight, that flicker of light was back inside of me. It wasn't worth it to feel that light again, knowing that living my truth outwardly would disappoint her and others in my life.

With full sincerity and caring, she walked me toward the exit and left me with these words, "You made a commitment to a man, and you need to honor that commitment and work harder at your marriage." My newly opened closet door was slammed and nailed shut. My perfectionist mode was engaged. I told myself that I just needed to work harder to be a good wife. I had put my truth out there to someone else and that had to be enough. I had freed myself of the black hole that gnawed at my insides for so long. Now I had a marriage to make better.

DRIFTING

Couples get bored. Lives become routine. Marriages get stale. My aunt shared with me that she and her husband slept in separate beds. I knew my grandparents used to do that too. And so did Fred and Wilma Flintstone. Even cartoons couldn't escape the challenges of being partnered for years.

My most recent craniosacral therapy session encouraged me to work harder at my marriage. Chris and I had started to more closely resemble roommates and best buds in recent years. We had never been wildly crazy lovebirds like some couples I knew, but the excitement we once felt had long since flown the coop. I hoped my sexuality wasn't the culprit. I recalled a female family member once describing sex as the "wifely duty." The term made me want to gag at the thought of being obligated to do anything physical. But it also signaled that perhaps a lot of women didn't enjoy sex and that maybe it was just one necessary piece that came along with marriage territory.

I had definitely put more boundaries around the level of intimacy I could handle each year, but maybe all women did that too.

Couldn't we just drift because that's what was supposed to happen in marriage? If we were following the "supposed to" path, then fixing things would be easier, wouldn't it?

Now clearly, I have a flair for life dramatics to solve problems. Don't like your hometown? Spend a year in Cochabamba. Upset about auditing a coal mine? Become a massage therapist. Fear you might be 50 shades of gay? Move abroad to a Catholic island. Marriage getting stale? Open a bar. Things don't work out? At least you have beer.

I hoped that I could reignite the flame of excitement between us by starting a business together. (In hindsight, who the heck ever says, "I know how to fix my marriage! I'll do it with entrepreneurship!") But having a bar was something Chris had always dreamed of, and I loved to see his inner light rekindle at the thought of making it a reality. I took that to mean that our relationship spark was back too.

A picture from an airplane magazine with a gorgeous golden snifter of beer and a small plate of savory food was all I needed to feel inspired. I had a vision now that this would be something good that we could bring to our community. We could support the local Florida craft beer scene that was starting to boom and bring back the feeling of those quaint shops that people yearned for in a city full of big retail chains. For the first time in a while, I saw his light flicker back with excitement.

Our Florida-focused craft beer bar and growler shop was positively received right from the beginning. Customers and breweries loved our concept. All our products came from other small businesses and supported the local economy. We featured taps with a variety of drinking options, including a gluten-free tap and two nonalcoholic taps with kombucha and coffee, so nobody felt excluded from having a social experience. We offered reusable glass growlers for beer-to-go, an environmentally friendly packaging option. We gave back generously to the community, donating hundreds of certificates for free pints to thirsty local schoolteachers. We weren't financially secure from the business, but we never lost money either. Our team was winning.

The bar also had somewhat of a shtick with our customers and on social media. Chris was the passionate, if somewhat disorganized, beer lover and bartending front man. I was the behind-the-scenes paper pusher and marketing speaker box that communicated all our events and kept Chris in line. Our bar was built on the foundation of family, both in the physical sense of our concrete handprints in the building's foundation and in our policies and way of operating. We were one of the only craft beer bars in Tampa at the time that offered free organic juice boxes in the fridge so that parents felt welcome to stop in and fill a growler, even if they had their kiddos in tow. A Tampa Bay magazine voted us one of the "Best Mom and Pop Shops," a colloquialism that makes me cringe now due to its exclusion of families who don't fit the traditional mold.

As the bar gained momentum, Chris became even more of the front man and I became even more of the behind-the-scenes gal. I knocked out work from the comfort of my fuzzy white bathrobe, squeezing in e-mails and merchandise orders between preparing and cleaning up snacks for the kids and trying to maintain somewhat of a homeschooling education. Watching "teaching cartoons" on Netflix suddenly became an acceptable school day to me. Entrepreneurship was harder than we expected.

In those early days of business, I used to wait anxiously for the bedroom door to open at the end of each night, staying awake until the wee hours for Chris to get home so I could spew all the adult words and stories that had accumulated in my mind during the day. It was mostly a one-sided conversation, as he attempted to end my gushing after all the adult socializing he had just done for hours in the bar. I needed connection. He needed a break.

More time passed, and eventually I got tired of my words falling on unresponsive ears. He was just tired. Too much work. Too little family time. Our relationship had drifted on and off for a while now, but adding the business only seemed to add a new layer of disconnect. For holidays and special occasions, Chris would grab a gift bag and fill it with the lingerie and nighties he had bought for me over the years, most of which had never been worn. It became kind of a joke between us that would play out over and over. I'd laugh and shove the lacy, silky things into the back of my underwear drawer once again. He'd laugh as his hopes for physical connection were dashed once more. I had no desire for physical connection, particularly as my need for verbal connection was going unmet.

We grew more distant, using all of our waking time together to discuss business over a hot, steamy espresso. Then he would leave and I would stay home, and we'd repeat the pattern the next day. I began to see him so infrequently that I started to wonder if this was what single parenthood was like. I had round-the-clock care of our kids and nearly complete responsibility for the interior maintenance of the home: all meals, all health care, all education, all extracurriculars . . . and somehow had to fit my work hours in as well. It was a juggling act where I was constantly dropping at least a third of the balls. But from the outside, nobody seemed to notice that I was a crappy juggler.

My friends would sprinkle me with comments like, "I don't know how you do it all!" or "Where do you find time in your day?" Meanwhile, I knew that we were having pasta with butter for dinner for the fourth night in a row or that we had skipped hairbrushing for the day, because pasta was easy and brushing was not. Exhaustion took up permanent residence in the depths of my bones. I wished someone would come in and toss me a lifesaver every now and then. I wondered if anyone else could see I was drowning in this life I had created, slowly slipping under the waves of responsibility with just enough buoyancy to suck in oxygen through the smile I wore in front of others.

I wondered if there was such a thing as appearing *too* capable. It was a perfectionist's dilemma: continue carrying on in a way so that everyone around you thinks you're fine and everything is a-okay, thus preserving your ego, or admit that you can't do it all, wave the white flag, and ask for help. Asking for help would have been the admission that I failed. My fragile ego wouldn't let me ask for help. Meanwhile, I hoped by some miracle that someone would come to my rescue without my asking for it.

My mom would send a care package to my brother in Denver when illness or misfortune seemed to come his way. I wished she saw the need in me as I stood right in front of her. My friends would take turns shuttling each other's kids to activities or babysitting when one had too much on her plate. I loved seeing the support and camaraderie, wondering if anyone would notice that maybe I also had too much on my plate. The facade I had built around myself, the story that everyone knew of me, was apparently too strong. Nobody knew my insides.

Sometimes I would watch Chris on the bar security cameras in the late hours of the night or early hours of the morning, long past closing time, drinking a beer and watching sports highlights on TV. I could see his physical exhaustion in the way his shoulders rolled forward, letting the bar's concrete countertop absorb the weight of his arms and the day. I would wonder when I would get a break to just sit there and be responsible to nobody except myself. But I couldn't fault him or feel jealous of him. I could see he was drowning in life too.

Reframe, I told myself. Our life was good, and we had so much going for us. The kids were alive. They were eating and learning and, most importantly, feeling loved. My ego relished the fact that outwardly I was appearing to prove that I could have it all: keep the home, care for the kids, run the business, have the marriage, style my hair in something other than a ponytail on occasion. The truth was that I realized I would need to find ways to take care of myself before I combusted into a ball of flames at the next homeschool meetup. And because my kids are both weird and oddly resourceful, they would probably roast homemade organic marshmallows over my flaming carcass.

I began to savor my quiet time home alone at night after the kids had gone to sleep and before Chris would lumber through the door and crash into bed. It was a few hours just for me. Sometimes I used those hours to put on a restorative yoga video and work on my breathing while drinking alkaline water. More often I would make myself a huge bowl of kids' cereal and binge-watch tattoo reality shows. This was that self-care that everyone said we should be doing. I rationalized that having a few unproductive hours in my day was necessary for my health, even if it involved a cereal box with a cartoon character on it. "They're always after me Lucky Charms" could have been my new self-care mantra. I was starting to get better. Our relationship was not.

Despite my efforts to want to work at our marriage, opening a bar was not the vehicle to do that. I mistook having a reinvigorated excitement for life as being a reinvigorated excitement for love. It's not. We were both stressed and exhausted, pouring our energy into an entity that we loved rather than pouring our time into loving each other. Even still, I didn't know if I truly wanted to work on our love.

I knew he loved me. I knew I had barriers around how completely I was able to love him. Working on our relationship would mean facing my fears surrounding my sexuality. I would either have to explore and accept the truth about myself, which would most likely prove disastrous to our marriage, or make the conscious decision to lie to myself to preserve the relationship we had. Tell the truth and end things. Live a lie to save things. Neither option felt good. I kept hoping that the bar would fill the empty space in him where my love was lacking and that maybe we'd never have to address our relationship at all.

When Chris came home at the end of the night, I no longer anxiously waited up, hoping to share every detail of my day. I knew it wasn't what he wanted, and it was no longer what I wanted either. I started to pretend that I had drifted off to sleep. It was just easier for both of us.

NETFLIX AND JILL

The strongest gaydar signals exist in the algorithms of the Internet. Netflix, Google, Facebook, and TikTok know the truth in your soul. They sense you're queer before you do. I often wonder to myself if having Lesbian TikTok at this point in my life would have helped expedite the process or made things more confusing. The isolation of the pandemic in 2020, coupled with a sudden abundance of lesbian videos on the app, led to a new tidal wave of women questioning whether they were really as straight as they assumed. But in 2018, we were still a few years from COVID-19 shaking the world. I didn't have TikTok, but I did have Netflix, and it was almost as good.

I started my evening binges with standard sitcom fare and the occasional documentary about mushrooms or Mexican prisons. But then Netflix decided to get cute. One night it suggested *The L Word* on my home screen. I looked around the room for spy cameras or some guy in a Netflix T-shirt standing outside my window with binoculars.

How did they know? Why would they suggest this? Was I allowed to watch this? Would watching this be enough to satisfy me for now? For the long haul? I hit play and began the binge.

Aside from the overexaggerated and often implausible storylines of *The L Word,* it brought me into a new world and way of life. Women. Out and proud lesbians. Drinking coffee and living in nice homes and fighting and loving and just existing in their own bubble of fabulousness, where all the bills got paid and they only had to work a few hours a month at their interesting careers. They went on dates. They had long-term relationships and cohabitated. It was the constant reminder to my brain that this was a valid thing. Women *could* live this way. I *could* live this way . . . minus the fancy home, fancy coffee, fancy daycare, and everything else fancy. (Perhaps it should have been called *The F Word).*

"Maybe in my next lifetime," I promised myself, hoping that I was betting on the right horse with my belief in reincarnation. At this point, I had become content with the thought that I could remain in my marriage for the rest of my life but give myself the permission to internally acknowledge the fact that I wasn't straight.

The L Word also added a new dimension to my queerness in a way I hadn't acknowledged before. It showed me how easily I could be turned on. While in the past I had my daydreams to try and envision what women's sexual interactions might be like, Netflix was showing it to me plain as day. It was one thing for me to think about two women being together. It was another thing to see it. To see them touch. To see them kiss. I remember the opening episode of *The L Word,* where Jenny Schecter peeks between the fence at her neighbor's house to find Shane (a highly coveted lesbian) and another woman skinny-dipping and making out in the pool. My heart raced. Every cell of my body came alive. I wanted that.

In my many evenings alone, I pored through episodes on my laptop, making sure to erase the watch history before the kids would log on for morning cartoons. When *The L Word* was done, I realized there were more lesbian films to color my life. *Blue Is the Warmest Color, Room in Rome,* and *Below Her Mouth* provided more sex education over the next few years than in my entire previous life. I became a student who studied the connection and closeness between the women in each movie. Their emotional swings were dynamic, but in those moments of tenderness, just lying together in comfort, my own body felt starved. I had snuggled before. I had spooned before. But I never felt the total surrender with another person that I saw on-screen. I wondered if it was just because these were movies or if that was something attainable in real life. I guessed that I would never know.

You would think that by this point my acknowledgment of myself as a lesbian would have been clear as day, but it wasn't. I could acknowledge *The L Word* on the screen but would not let that L word become part of my own identity. I couldn't picture a life without Chris, our business, or our family under one roof. I couldn't picture a world where I would feel a pull strong enough to put everything I knew at risk to enter a new and unknown life. The words from my mom, that life would be harder, still echoed in my thoughts. I had to reconcile that although I may be queer, I was not willing to sacrifice anything to live that truth out.

So, I came up with ways that I thought would honor myself without taking me out of my safe zone. I hung a crystal from the rearview mirror in my car. As the Florida sun shone through the glass, rainbows would party across my dashboard and seats. Bonus points if Gavin DeGraw's "In Love With a Girl" or Katy Perry's "I Kissed a Girl" came on the radio. I would smirk, singing along, and catch the rainbows on my skin. Those moments felt blissful.

And then I would return to my reality and life would start to feel heavy again. Finding so much joy in those moments only made the knowledge that this was as far as I was willing to go cut all the deeper. I was okay thinking I may be gay. I was not okay with anyone else thinking it.

Although I wasn't ready to admit it, I had internalized homophobia. The revelation that I was "okay" with gay people but not at all okay with me identifying as a gay person shook me. When it came down to it, I had my own hierarchy of relationships, and queer ranked below hetero. When it came to perception of self, I saw my queerness as a failure or flaw. There was no such thing as being "perfectly queer." I was figuring out a painful lesson. Being homophobic was not reserved for the loud people with neon posters who protested at Pride events and Drag Queen Story Hours. Homophobia, by definition, was a fear of same-sex feelings and relationships. I had a new layer of unpacking around why I didn't see love as love and why my queerness was not part of my identity that I could love.

Maybe it's my perfectionism. Maybe it's my tendency to dive with gusto headfirst into problems. Regardless of the cause, I was committed to reeducating myself, if for no other reason than my own self-preservation. I had to grow my love for the LGBTQ+ community if I had any shot at growing love for myself. I hit the books, ready to replace any negative thoughts of the LGBTQ+ that had been sown within me with seeds of positivity and pride.

I studied the history of queer celebrations and important LGBTQ+ advocates. I read articles and watched interviews about Ellen DeGeneres coming out on her sitcom and why it was so monumental. I studied the AIDS epidemic, which I was only moderately familiar with as a teen in the early '90s. I realized that I had little understanding of the pain and community-wide fear caused by the Pulse nightclub shooting in Orlando. In the past, it was all just news headlines to me. Now I was putting myself in their shoes. Now I felt the stories viscerally.

This was a new way of joining the queer community. It wasn't just surrounding myself with queer people while enjoying the privileges of heterosexual life. I was going to become, at the very least, a strong ally. I unlearned phrases like *sexual preference* and exchanged them for *sexual orientation*. Terms like *tranny* that were still being spewed on TV I relearned as *transgender*. I learned that some people were okay with *queer* as gay culture reclaimed the word, while others were still very sensitive to it (and rightfully so). I read stories of what it meant to be pansexual, demisexual, intersex, asexual, aromantic, nonbinary, and gender-nonconforming, and why some prefer the pronouns *ze/zem* or other variations I was unaware of. I wanted to be better and do better, even among a group that I never saw myself being outwardly a part of. "Love them to love yourself," I repeated.

One of the most common questions I get today is, "When did you know you were gay?" I find that many queer people struggle with having a definitive time frame. Frankly, I think if you asked most heterosexual people, "When did you know you were straight?" they would have a hard time answering with a definitive time frame too.

But maybe that's because they never had to question their sexuality. It was always just assumed for them.

What complicates the answer for me is that there are really two parts to that question: knowing, but also accepting. The knowing and the accepting I find to be inextricably linked. I suppose I could say that technically I "knew" I was some letter of the LGBTQIA for a long time. Perhaps you could even say my knowing started back in third grade when I knew I liked another girl.

However, it's missing the vital piece that is acceptance. Acceptance is believing what you know. I could know I might be or probably was gay, but if I couldn't accept that about myself, then it would never feel true. Acceptance is adoption of that truth as part of my identity. For a long time, I knew. But at age 37 I was still not fully ready to accept. A "heterosexual ally" would remain how I identified myself to the rest of the world. That was all I could handle. That was all I was ready to accept.

The incongruity of what I felt about myself internally and who I would allow myself to be externally hurt. It was like the harder my soul tried to burst out, the more staunchly I shoved it down inside of me, covering it with duct tape and superglue so that it would stay in its spot. I wondered how long I would have to go on in my uncomfortable human suit living like this.

TOES AND A CEMETERY TOMBSTONE

Their toes. I remember that's what struck me most. It was the way they gently rested together, one foot barely touching the other. The sheet under the lower foot was puckered, as if that foot had pulled it up to greet the other one so delicately. My heart clenched. I wasn't a voyeur. They were made of marble.

One benefit to homeschooling my children is that we take a ton of field trips. Homeschooling forces me to be a tourist in my own town and visit places that I wouldn't normally go. My eight- and five-year-old were accompanying me and a gaggle of other homeschoolers to the Tampa Museum of Art to see Yayoi Kusama's traveling exhibit *Love is Calling*. I said a little prayer that no expensive paintings would get licked.

We reached Kusama's work, a trippy and whimsical mirrored room. Brightly colored squiggly stalagmites and stalactites protruded from the ceiling and floor. They were covered in black dots. The room was dimly lit, making the illusion even more intense. It was like we entered a Dr. Seuss world that perhaps director Tim Burton had added his own dark flair to. Magical and weird. Our group entered and exited the mirrored box room. The consensus seemed to be "whoa."

We were quickly ushered into the next room to allow the growing line of patrons to enter the Kusama exhibit and have their own piece of whoa. That's when I had my moment. In front of me was an oversized marble slab of two people lying in bed together. It was stunning.

I looked around me nervously, like I had just walked in on an intimate bedroom scene that I wasn't supposed to have viewed. My kids were happily distracted with their friends and didn't seem to be at risk of breaking or eating any ancient artifacts. I returned my gaze to the marble. One figure was nestled into the nook of the other's arm, one side-lying and one face up. Just resting. The sheets of stone over them looked so soft, like they were freshly draped across the figures' waists and thighs. And there was the most serene look on the face-up figure's lips as if to say, "I'm home."

Then I got closer and realized that the two figures, wrapped in a sweet and comforting embrace, were both women. Ack! I was caught in the act of lesbian voyeurism. I scanned the room again for anyone who may have noticed I was overattentive to Patricia Cronin's sculpture. Nobody seemed to notice or care but me.

I sunk back into the sculpture, titled *Memorial to a Marriage*, and read the description: "Unveiled in 2002 at the Woodlawn Cemetery in the Bronx, *Memorial to a Marriage* was Cronin's celebration in death of her marriage to partner, Deborah Kass, that could not be made legal in life." A lump came to my throat.

While marriage for queer couples finally became federally legal in the U.S. in 2015, I was transported back 13 years prior to when the sculpture was created. My heart hurt to see these two figures together, so clearly in love, not have society acknowledge them for who they were and what they felt between them. I wanted to give Patricia and Deborah a hug. And then I wanted to paint a sign and go protest somewhere . . . anywhere . . . that a love this pure should never have been a crime.

I snapped a quick picture of Cronin's Carrara marble sculpture so that I wouldn't forget it. Like I could forget it. Looking at that sculpture was just a reminder of what I would never have. I was still completely committed to staying in my marriage to Chris. And yet, here I was staring at a carving of two women—I felt myself choke with emotion.

I will never have that, I told myself. The weight of that realization was as heavy as stone. Denying myself this type of connection and this type of love now felt like dragging an invisible ball and chain with me throughout my day. I wondered if carrying this weight would make me stronger over the years, confirming my conviction to make my marriage and the commitment to my family work. If Glennon Doyle's famous phrase "We can do hard things" had been out in the world at this time, I would have convinced myself that *this* was my hard thing, my burden to bear in this life. And look at me! Look how well I was managing. A+ Jill. You get to live the rest of your life with a chronic case of hetero. Way to suffer!

But that is not what Doyle meant. Her "hard things" were forward motion, even if the steps were small and required rest. Her "hard things" meant being honest with oneself and making the difficult choices to move toward a more beautiful life. But in that time, there with those two marble figures, I was convinced that my self-sacrifice was the path I was supposed to be on. Despite the number of flights I had been on in my lifetime, for some reason my mind kept telling me to put on everyone else's oxygen mask first before I put on my own.

It's funny to me. On a plane, nobody would ever question me if I did things the way they advised and put on my own mask first. Everyone would know that if I didn't put my mask on first, I ran the very real risk of passing out before I could be there to help those around me. Why do we struggle with taking that aviation concept back to our lives on the ground? The flight attendant wasn't saying, "Hey girl, hey! Put on your mask and then recline your seat and sip your overpriced Bloody Mary while you watch those around you try to figure things out!" It was just the simple request that when your survival needs are met, you can better attend to the needs of those around you. When you are cared for, you can better care for others.

I wondered why that concept seemed so easy to comprehend on a plane but didn't get applied in the same way elsewhere. And why were women and mothers most often the ones who were shamed or seen as selfish if we did put ourselves first? Were we not the ones who most often had to care for others? Did we not deserve to be cared for as a priority in our daily lives, so that we would have the ability to care for them?

It's a simple concept, really. But for me, standing there in that museum, I saw my two lives in front of me. I saw my vulnerable children running around the museum floor with their friends, carefree and happy. I saw me being able to be there with them because my husband's paycheck afforded me the benefit of not having to work a traditional job. And I saw Cronin's sculpture, two people so profoundly in love that even in cold stone the warmth of their connection radiated outward. It was love on all levels: the physical, the emotional, the energetic, the spiritual. They filled the dark corners inside of me that seemed empty.

Two yearnings stood before me that day. My heart ached deeply for both. My mind told me I could only have one.

STAGE THREE

RAPID DECLINE

SELF-LOVEIVERSARY

It was July 3rd, Independence Day eve in the United States.

"Do you have a person?" she asked me.

My face was soaked with a healthy layer of salty tears as I sat on the side of her therapy table, hugging a small glass of water in both of my hands. "No," I whispered, taking a shaky sip. Her sun-kissed skin melted into a warm smile as she put a hand on my shoulder. "Then there is nothing you need to do right now." My heart lifted. She was right. This was not a time for action. There was nothing I needed to do right now.

Ninety minutes prior, I had arrived at Agnieszka's office for CST. It was a reunion of sorts. I had taken the kids for therapy but passed on taking care of myself for a while, because that's what moms tend to do. Today I felt overdue.

Her office was a small, clay-colored building surrounded by vibrant Florida vegetation, wind chimes, and reflective mirrors. Inside, the room was a serene gray blue. The building looked fiery and wild on the outside, with total peace on the inside. I grinned. It was the inverse of how my body felt on most days.

I didn't go into the session with a plan. I rarely do. I knew that Agnieszka was talented enough and neutral enough to let my body lead and work through whatever it needed on that day. It was always a bit scary to hop on that table. I always felt incredibly vulnerable not knowing where the session would go, but I had complete faith in my own body to heal in the way that it needed and in the timing that it needed. My mind briefly wondered if I would reveal the truth of my sexuality again. Nearly six years had passed since my admission of bisexuality; perhaps that would come up again. I brushed it off. My sexual orientation was not a priority to me, and I thought I already had answered myself. Yes, you can be gay. Just not in this lifetime.

The session began like any other: Agnieszka rested her hands gently on the tops of my feet, tracked the points in my body that needed attention, and then moved to each one, making what I call "a hand sandwich" over the area. When I could feel myself getting uncomfortable, I might start to chat and crack a dad joke. I would call these moments "a hand sandwich with cheese." She continued working on different points of my body until her hand sandwich ended up over the spot. *The spot.* The black hole from six years ago. I thought that wound had healed and here she was, right over it.

You can tell her, popped into my mind. *Tell her what?* I argued back at myself. *You're gay!* my self responded. I tensed. She felt it. Obviously she felt it.

"What's going on here?" Agnieszka asked in a soft Polish accent, with more curiosity than prying. I knew I wasn't obligated to answer. I chose to stay quiet. I felt the heat rushing to my face as I scrunched up my nose and lips in an effort to hold back the rising emotions. I couldn't stop my eyes from getting glassy.

The mental tug-of-war continued. *I'm not doing this again,* I yelled to myself. *You can tell her,* I reassured myself. My mind flashed back again to my CST session of years prior. I couldn't go through the rejection again, knowing that a second cut like that would scar even deeper. *She is safe,* my body assured me.

I shut my eyes tighter, like I could implode into my eyeballs and disappear if I squeezed hard enough. And then I relaxed into the truth. This wasn't going away. I couldn't implode into nothing. And despite my best efforts to padlock the closet door of my sexual orientation, I was also gifting myself the key. I promised to unlock the closet door with one condition: this time I would say my actual truth.

"I'm . . . I'm . . . " I took a deep breath. The next word would be a game changer in my life. A pivot point where my identity was about to take a sharp turn.

"I'm . . . gay."

"That's wonderful," she replied.

I had said it. I had meant it. And I was okay.

My memory may be a bit foggy after that, but I am pretty sure that 99 angels descended from the sky with harps and flutes and all that extraneous angel band equipment, like kazoos and glockenspiels. They were surrounding me in white light as I had an out-of-body experience.

That didn't happen, but what did came close. I felt love. Real, true, profound, deep love. Like the love you feel when you look into your baby's, or your soulmate's, or your Chihuahua's eyes. A year later, when a life coach asked me to recall my strongest memory of feeling unconditional love, it was this moment. Pure, profound love. What I didn't realize in that moment, though, was that the unjudged love I felt wasn't coming from Agnieszka. This was that unconditional self-love that everyone talks about. That elusive holy grail, the thing for which hundreds of books have been written; yet determining how to feel that love remained out of reach. I always thought I had self-love because I told myself I did. Now I knew what it really felt like.

I loved myself. I loved my *whole* self. I loved that dark part of me where shame and fear had resided. I was gay. I loved myself for that. I loved Agnieszka for seeing that and loving it too. It was like energetic love Ping-Pong balls around the room, and I felt so very good. I had said it. The truth. I'm gay. And I loved myself for it.

For those hung up on the "When did you know?" aspect of coming out, this was my true knowing that was now paired with acceptance. I had been scared, in the past, of how my life would change if I ever reached the point of knowing and accepting. In this moment, on Independence Day eve, that shift had occurred. My soul ripped off the duct tape and rose up, filling every corner of my body. I felt solid and secure. I celebrate July 3rd every year as my Self-Loveiversary.

Unfortunately, it didn't take long for the rational mind to tap me on the shoulder in my moment of bliss and turn my insides back to loose sand. As I got my weary body upright at the end of the session, my mind went to one person. The tears started all over again. Chris. My husband. I was gay. This was the truth, and now I knew it and trusted it and accepted it. Shit. Now what? Now what do I do? Oh my God . . . oh my God . . . now what?! My tears turned to panic at the realization of what had just happened. My hands trembled around the glass of water Agnieszka had poured for me.

"Do you have a person?" she asked me. I didn't. There was nobody I was looking to date. No person I had fallen for in that moment to make me realize I was gay and wanted to be with them. I've learned from others in my new community that this was actually pretty rare. More commonly, people who come out in life do so because they find an overwhelming attraction to someone and want to pursue a relationship. That person is their catalyst—*the* person who helps transform and confirm their knowing. Often these relationships don't work out, perhaps due to the intensity and major identity shift that occurs during them. But sometimes they do, and it's the start of an incredible love story. Real-life love at first sight. I had always wondered if that was really a thing.

Regardless, I didn't have a person. I didn't even have any potential prospects in mind. I hoped that maybe someday I'd find somebody who also found themselves attracted to me—a middle-aged, minivan-driving, homeschooling mom who had only been in one serious relationship with a man her entire life. Did such a person who would be attracted to me and my story exist? I didn't know. But today, right now, it was just me. Alone. Freshly birthed, baby gay Jill.

I understand why most babies cry at birth. You leave comfort and security, are evicted from the life you've always known, and have no idea where the hell you are in this new space. It's terrifying. I wanted somebody to wrap me in a blanket and just hold me tight. But here I was, born into this new identity without a lover's arms calling me toward them. I was grateful that at least I had Agnieszka's support. I would need that safety net of community and friendship around me.

In life, waiting can be painful. Waiting for test results. Waiting for a plane to arrive. Waiting for a verdict. Waiting for dinner to be done. But time is also a gift, if we can view it as such. In the coming-out process, time means the ability to process the many life changes that have and will occur. Time would allow me to slowly sink into my new identity, try it on for size, rather than being pushed into the center spotlight of gossip among family, friends, and acquaintances who would feel a right to an opinion about whether or not my identity was valid and okay for me to have. I was going to need strength for the road ahead, and time allowed me to go inward and sit with myself. I had to get to know my new identity so that I could stand strongly in it. Time is a gift that is not afforded to many in the coming-out process. I now understand why it is so painful and inappropriate to "out" another person. You rob them of time.

I didn't know if I had any more courage left in me to come out to anyone else again. But at least, in that moment, I didn't have to. Now I could be deliberate about who I would let know and when I would let them know. This was the beginning of a long journey of a million tiny steps.

WORLD-CHAMPION WIFE

Orlando, Florida . . . or what I affectionately refer to as "Little Kids' Vegas." Chris, the kids, and I checked into a massive chain hotel that I had booked months early for the Tiger-Rock Martial Arts World Championship. The kids and I would be competing against other tae kwon do competitors from Tiger-Rock schools located in exotic locales like South Dakota and Georgia. The tournament title made me grin, as I equated it to the Super Bowl winners considering themselves "World Champions" in a competition that no other countries compete in. *U.S. takes it again!* I thought to myself.

The Jill who had just started tae kwon do 11 months prior would have never competed in this tournament. She would have shown up with a bag full of applesauce pouches, energy bars, and water with dissolved minerals, as she reminded her children for the 1,387th time that their body would absorb it better and they'd pee less.

But that was a different Jill. That was the Jill who got goaded into taking tae kwon do by the school owner, Nikki, who said, "Parents train free. So, you can either sit there and just watch your kids every week or you can get a workout in your day." She appealed to my inner frugality and "I'll show you!" spirit.

Tae kwon do was my *Fear Factor*—the thing I had wanted to do ever since I found out my high school friend Ashley had achieved the rank of black belt in her youth. I would hype myself up into trying to take a class, only to come up with a short laundry list of excuses for why I wasn't a good fit. Mainly, (1) I didn't want to get kicked or punched, and (2) I just wasn't the martial arts "type." I pictured myself sticking out in class like peaceful PBS painter Bob Ross at a death metal concert.

That's why I shocked myself that July when I was signed up to compete in the tournament as a freshly belted Blue Level 1. I would be competing with other adult women in their 20s and older, all within the same color belt rank, and I was stoked to do it. Those previous months of training had turned me from a reluctant minivan mom who was nearly to the point of vomiting at the thought of doing her Ho-Am form in front of the class, to an empowered woman who could do more push-ups than she had ever been capable of and had a respectable set of abs. I wasn't "mom" or "wife" on the mat. I was just Jill—and I felt brave.

Coming out to Agnieszka just a few weeks prior only further emboldened this sense of lesbian badassery. Aside from the looming fear of what the future inevitably held related to my family, I took the present time to revel in my newfound self-love and empowerment. I cut my hair short into a sharply angled bob that whipped around when I snapped a knife-hand strike. My voice opened up more, too, in what felt like a physical change. Whereas in the past I would feel a pressure in my throat whenever I made a feeble attempt to swear, discuss things like menstruation, or name body parts without cheesy nicknames, I found that all of my words could just come out now. Words weren't swallowed, they now flowed freely at my command. When I yelled "ay" in tae kwon do, it no longer came out sounding like a question but rather a bold statement of "I am here!" It was the start of finding my voice.

I won big that day, with Chris and my children cheering me on, and proudly walked home with six medals around my neck for board breaking, forms, and sparring. One of them was the silver Masters medal for forms, meaning that I ranked number 2 among all competitors in my age range and rank level at the tournament. "I'm a silver medalist at the World Championship." I giggled to myself as I strolled my achy body back to the hotel and prepared to take my kids out to whatever restaurant had chicken tenders on the menu.

When I got back to the hotel, Chris told me he had a surprise for me. He was so proud of my kick-ass performance that day that he upgraded our hotel room to a suite. The kids would have their own bedroom and we would have privacy. I could see the twinkle in his eyes at what that meant for the evening. He was proud of me. He was in love with me and what I had accomplished that day. He was turned on by me. I felt a lump return to my throat.

We had sex that night. It was our usual quickie, where I didn't make eye contact and didn't allow touch to nearly all parts of my body. The only thing that didn't make it usual was the fact that I now understood why I rarely enjoyed sex. I knew at that point that I never would, or could, go back to enjoying sex with him. It wasn't who I was. However, until I was ready to vocalize my truth to him, I now had a role to play in our marriage.

Check the box. "Wifely duty" satisfied.

NOT STRAIGHT

Jack Daniel's Tennessee Honey whiskey is a dangerous drink. You never know when you'll be peacefully sipping a glass of it on the rocks with your dearest friend in her kitchen, chatting about park days and meal plans, and annoying things husbands do . . . and then BAM, you're a blubbery, red-faced ball of tears confessing your soul's deepest fear. That is what Jack does (they just leave that warning off the bottle).

Tisa (rhymes with *Lisa*) had been my nearest and dearest pal over the past three years. We met at a bounce house place in 2016 and were the only two parents there. Since Tisa is an extrovert, and I hate to appear rude by running screaming into a quiet corner, we conversed while our kids bounced their excessive energy away. Tisa also gives really good advice, even to strangers. I confessed my struggles with my daughter's education in public school, she told me to homeschool, and so I did.

Year after year this pattern continued. I had a problem that seemed insurmountable, and Tisa tuned in with her supersonic listening skills, undistracted by phone dings and children falling off trampolines. Then she dispensed sage words of wisdom. She helped when I was venting about my mom and whatever boundary she was trying to take a chainsaw to at the moment. She helped when I was trying to figure out how to get a chartreuse couch I impulsively bought off the Facebook marketplace back to my home. She helped when my son, Ollie, seemed to be exhibiting some neurodivergent tendencies. So it's no surprise that she would be the first non-therapist (or I should say unpaid therapist) that I would divulge my secret to.

But sharing my life-altering, soul-freeing truth with her was not actually part of my plan. In hindsight, the thought of keeping this information from her seems ridiculous because she is quite possibly the most perfect person in the world to share it with. But that wasn't part of my plan. No sharing. Not ever. Not with anyone other than the therapist I was actually paying. Not even with Tisa. For some reason, I felt like I had already done enough and would be okay having told two different therapists my two different truths. I felt like, since the words had exited my mouth and were into the universe, that would be enough to go on with my happy daily life.

The problem was, I now knew what was "wrong" with me. Nothing. Nothing was wrong with me. I was perfectly whole. That realization became a seed of truth that was now planted in my soul, and that seed wanted to grow. I could feel the roots of my truth begin to innervate my insides. Its tendrils curled up around my brain and bloomed in my thoughts. As I became filled with my truth, I realized a very scary thing. Keeping this truth inside of my body pot was going to cause root rot. Just like a real plant, it would become unhealthy and would wither and die if it didn't get the proper space and nourishment it needed.

Fun fact . . . I have no green thumb. Not with real plants, and certainly not with propagating the soul seeds of truth that grow through my body. So I opted for the "keep it in and let it die" approach. Because the thing about this truth plant is that not everyone would find it beautiful. I knew I was going to risk a lot of "Whoa! What happened to you?" or "How did we not know that you had this plant growing within you?!" Or worse, "That is a disgusting plant, and you should be ashamed!" I knew that the moment the pot broke open, my easy, happy world might break apart as well. My relationship of 18 years would be done. I might lose my kids. I might lose our house. I might lose my business. Faced with a wide-open future full of potentially horrible unknowns, keeping my secret felt safer. Even keeping it from Tisa, who would say, "Come here, you beautiful weirdo," and embrace me with open arms. It was terrifying.

That's where our good pal Jack Daniel's comes in. I'm not much of a drinker, but that night in Tisa's kitchen, while the children ran amok like beautiful, feral homeschoolers, a glass of Jack's Honey Whiskey on the rocks felt like just the thing I needed to temporarily pause that then constant feeling of fear that had become part of my daily life. So we sipped and talked, and sipped and talked. I listened to her vent about her marriage frustrations and fears. And then she said, "How are you and Chris?"

That was it. The magical words that made the pot crack and forced my insides to slowly start leaking out in the form of tears and a now Rudolph-red nose. My brain started to fight me on telling her what was really going on, but good ol' Jackie boy punched back at those brain cells and the words fumbled out of my mouth.

"I'm . . . not . . . straight!" I choked out, followed by more tears than I knew my body was capable of producing. I don't recall the exact words she said, just that her jaw kind of dropped and her eyes grew wide. I think she uttered something to the extent of "Wow! Not what I was expecting. I thought you were going to say he was cheating on you, and I was about ready to beat him up." (That's a true friend there.) And then, she seemed almost happy, or maybe she was proud of me, or maybe she had gas. Regardless, the most genuine, caring smile crossed her face, and I knew that I was going to be okay. She liked my plant. I felt like I had just received permission to bloom.

I wish I had been the journaling type of lesbian back then and had written down exactly how our conversation went. The truth of the matter is my brain turned to total mush, just as it has done over and over again every time I've come out to a new person. The extreme fear turns to elation, and love, and my brain seems to shut down from the shock of it all.

That conversation is funny to me in hindsight because not once did I use the term *lesbian*—I just couldn't say it. I'm not even sure I said *gay* that night. *Not straight* was all I could offer. It made me realize that maybe I wasn't all of a sudden okay and accepting of my gayness just because I had said it in therapy. This was only the start of my next journey, my new life. I was quickly watching the story I had written over the past 38 years close, hoping that the next book to come would not be a total horror story, and that it would hopefully have some sort of happy ending. Either way, there was no going back now. I was not straight, and the outside world was starting to know.

CAFFEINE DEATH SPIRALS

Unfortunately, the happiness high of coming out to Agnieszka had long since worn off. The hollow space inside of me was back and I didn't know how to fill it. Being able to come out to myself was a huge challenge; I always thought it would be my biggest challenge, as I was my worst critic. I didn't want to belittle the bravery it took for me to admit my queerness to myself. But I quickly realized that the step of accepting myself was just a big first step in a long journey ahead.

Let me drop a metaphor on you to explain my life at this point. It was like skipping a stone (me) on a pond (life): the stone initially feels the impact of hitting the water (coming out), and then flies back up into the air for a bit of reprieve (dissociation), repeating this pattern a few more times. Eventually, though, the stone loses strength (coming out to a lot of people) and can no longer rebound off the water. It creates a splash (the big coming out) and then a large ripple that affects the surrounding water (people in my life), all while it sinks to the bottom. A fish (homophobic family member) might get scared in the process and ask the stone why it had the audacity to ever leave the shore (heterosexuality). The fish never saw that the hand of an unseen power (God/Source/the Universe) was the one that picked up that stone and propelled it forward. The stone was just along for the ride and hoped that one day some beautiful womanly soul (hot, sporty lesbian) would pluck her out of the muck (real life) and take her home (Maui) and love her (orgasms) and make her gluten-free chocolate-chip cookies (cookies with gluten) and call her *babe*.

Fine. So perhaps that metaphor is a bit of a stretch. At that time, though, my body and subconscious must have known that the harder trials lay ahead, while my brain was busy daydreaming about cookies and softball players. My body's first reaction to the trauma was insomnia. All day I would feel exhaustion from the toll of being a homeschooling mom and a business owner. My king-sized bed with a healthy smattering of pillows was my respite that then turned to just spite. I would crawl into my cozy bed, hoping to repair and restore from the tolls of the day. But then I was suddenly too hot. Then I was suddenly too cold. My fatigued corpse seemed to find every reason to not sleep. I would just lie there, staring at my white popcorn ceiling and wondering how messy it would really be to just scrape all of the popcorn off, while waiting to hear the doors to our house and the bedroom open as Chris got home from another late night at the bar. I wondered if pretending to be asleep would be almost as good as actually falling asleep. Sometimes sleep came. Often it didn't. I would look at Chris while he slept, delving deeper into dark thoughts of our future, while waiting anxiously for the sun to rise through the bedroom window and start another day.

Insomnia encouraged me to pursue a caffeine death spiral. My sunken eyes were barely open as I downed one or two strong Cuban espressos in the morning. This was followed by a mid-morning Cuban espresso to keep myself going until lunch. I remember I used to hold the tiny ceramic mug upside down at my lips, waiting for the last drop of precious bitter liquid to enter my system. Then I would pick up the remnants of Chris's cold morning espresso and also consume those final drops as well. There never seemed to be enough. The only thing that would stop me from making more was the feeling of my heart pounding so furiously that I worried it might pop like a balloon if I pushed my luck.

While the espresso did succeed in keeping me vertical during the day, it also sent my adrenal glands into overdrive. I felt jittery and unfocused. My dear pal Tisa, picked up on how angry too much caffeine seemed to make me. She suggested tea. I suggested she shut her well-intentioned face hole. I was not in a good place, made even worse by the fact that my body was starving itself. Another effect of the espresso—it seemed to suppress my already nonexistent appetite, thanks to the stress I was under. I had to force myself to make food go down my throat so that I had something to run off of, even if it was just a few tortilla chips or a mandarin orange. I knew that giving up the coffee might help break me out of this unhealthy spiral, but I also knew that if I did give it up, I might not have any energy to drag my wet-noodle body out of bed in the morning. Plus, it was one of the few things I looked forward to in that time. I couldn't put the small cup of deadly joy down.

I know it may be hard to believe, but my mental state was suffering as well. My drive to be the perfect parent, perfect business owner, perfect mom, and perfect daughter was severely weakening. Rather than admit failure and ask for help, I started to just tap out and disconnect. I felt like I couldn't be doing a bad job if I did no job at all.

I reduced my role in life to just the basics. I made sure the kids got fed and that their fingernails didn't grow to the length of falcon talons, but could offer little else to them at that time. We just snuggled in bed a lot together—them on their tablets, me keeping my mind occupied by hours of vapid social media scrolling without even comprehending the content I was looking at. We ate a lot of pasta and PB&J sandwiches, with a few baby carrots on the side "to be healthy." I couldn't bring myself to plan a meal or properly grocery shop, particularly when my own hunger was gone.

I starting doing the bare minimum I could to allow the bar to still operate. Bills got paid. Supplies got ordered. Occasionally, I'd come up with something witty for social media. But my capacity to do anything beyond keeping the ship afloat was gone. I just couldn't make myself care anymore.

The lack of caring frightened me a bit. Was this what depression felt like? Was I losing my mind? For a brief blip, I contemplated if it would be easier on everyone if I ended my life rather than putting my family through the unavoidable future. Fortunately, that thought went away as quickly as it came. No self-arguing needed. I still had value here. *This is just a season,* I told myself in pep talks to remember that nothing in life stayed static.

Showers became my new hiding place where I could put on loud music and let the water cascade over me as I escaped from my own thoughts. In fact, loud music suddenly had to follow me everywhere: in the car, cooking breakfast in the morning, waiting for tae kwon do class to start. Headphones were nearly permanent fixtures in my ears. Chris noticed my newfound love of bathing and music and sweetly bought me a shower radio to enhance the sound quality. He never questioned my new habits or thinning frame. He knew I was busy. He knew I had a lot on my mind.

What I didn't realize at the time was that I was experiencing dissociation, what Nicole LePera describes in her book *How to Do the Work* as "a coping mechanism of physical and mental disconnection from our environment in response to consistent stress or overwhelm. A person is physically there but mentally gone."[2] *Hot damn,* I thought as I read that line a year later.

I wish her book had been published while I was going through this major life change. It offered so many beautiful insights into why I felt crazy and struggled to recognize the person I was and the way I was living. I laughed, thinking about the number of times my friends would talk to me, see my distant expression and say, "Oops . . . Jill's back on her cloud." What may have looked like me being uninterested, distant, or aloof was my mind's response to trying to make it through the day in one piece. I thank the sweet baby Jesus for patient and understanding friends who allowed me time in Cloudtown when I needed it.

I learned even more about dissociation from the book *What Happened to You?*, by Oprah Winfrey and Bruce D. Perry. It was eye-opening when I heard their advice years after my coming-out experience. Perry described dissociation as a way that our bodies respond to trauma that is different from fight-or-flight arousal. It serves an important purpose and allows us a much-needed rest from the current chaos, while releasing pain killers and endorphins. Dissociation allows us to flee to our inner world when the trauma of our outer world becomes too much.

I wish I had known this back then, instead of beating myself up for feeling lazy. I wish I could have given myself loving permission to take the time to retreat inward and seen it as a necessary part of the healing process rather than selfish care. I wish I had known that I wasn't crazy. I wish I had known that feeling the way I felt was part of the process. I wish I had realized that the changes in my brain and body were a physiological stress response. I wasn't losing my mind. I wasn't doing this in a vain attempt to reclaim my youth, like the "midlife crisis" that some would use to try and explain away my sexual revelation. I was experiencing trauma while simultaneously refusing to allow myself to identify it as such.

Coming out can be a traumatic experience that starts long before letting others in on your truth. It doesn't matter how much you love yourself, how good it feels to come out, and how supported you are by your friends and family. Coming out can be a traumatic identity shift. It took me years before I could admit that. How could something I wanted for myself be considered traumatic? Was this really trauma if I was choosing to put myself in a traumatic situation? How could something that felt as good and freeing as loving oneself also cause so much pain?

I was scared to attach any negativity to my coming-out experience. I felt that if I could stay happy in it, then others would naturally have to be happy for me. I rationalized that if I had any negative feelings, then I was signaling to myself and others that acknowledging my queerness was not actually something I wanted. I thought that if I wanted to be loved and accepted, I had to be the most loving and accepting of myself. I didn't want the dark cloud of trauma to mask my new rainbow life.

I didn't understand at the time that you can both celebrate your self-love and also grieve the person you once were. I didn't understand that I could feel such a lightness and joy when thinking about the fact that maybe, possibly, someday I would find a woman I could love with my whole heart, and also feel complete anguish and heartbreak at having to admit to my husband that I could never love him in that way . . . no matter how hard I tried. I didn't understand that feeling like I was losing my mind and withdrawing from the day-to-day routine was not me being lazy or selfish, it was my body's attempt at self-preservation and a response to the overwhelm I was experiencing. I didn't understand that I was allowed to feel both good and bad, high and low, happy and heartbroken all at the same time. At this point in my life, without yet knowing the work of LePera and Perry, I just felt crazy and alone.

GREATEST GIFT

Even Elton John married a woman. Elton John married a woman. I'm not the only one. Elton John once married a woman.

This was my mantra that I repeated at least 108 times per day. I did it to try and keep myself sane. In hindsight, it's probably the craziest possible rationalization for coming out later in life. But in my process, I felt so alone. I didn't know anyone locally who had ever done what I was doing. Nor regionally. Nor nationally. In fact, in this moment, the person I felt I had the most in common with was Sir Elton John himself. He sang about tiny dancers. I was a tiny dancer. We both liked sequins and had occasional diva meltdowns. Practically soul sisters. Sir Elton was also one of the most securely queer people I knew, and he had also been in a heterosexual marriage. To me, Elton John was Exhibit A that sometimes gay people could enter into straight relationships. I wouldn't be the first one on Earth.

Today there are countless resources, like Kari DeWitt's "Late Bloomer Lesbian+ Support Group" on Facebook, Robin Douglass's *Coming Out Late* podcast, and Lesbian TikTok. So many of us were going through the same thing around the same time. Even still, the universal theme of coming out seems to be similar for most: we all feel alone.

My brain peppered me with doubt daily. I questioned what being a lesbian meant. I never had to outwardly label myself as heterosexual, so the feeling of being labeled as anything at all felt odd. I questioned if that's how I wanted to identify and wanted others to identify me for the rest of my life. I still wasn't able to fully shake the negative connotation that had been attached to the word *lesbian* my whole life.

The annoying perfectionist troll in my mind would keep me occupied by saying things like, *Ewwww. You're really going to give up all of this just to "other" yourself in society?* and *Maybe you're* not *really sexually attracted to women. Maybe you* could *just be broken. Maybe* that *is your truth.* I didn't find the mind troll to be particularly witty or intelligent. But boy was she persistent.

Another aha moment from LePera's book came from her chapter "Ego Stories." She noted, "The more we deny parts of our shadow self, the more shame we feel and the more disconnected we become from our intuition."[3] I wish I had known that then. I couldn't understand why I could both continuously question my sexuality while also knowing more clearly than ever that I was a lesbian. It was a fierce match of internal Ping-Pong between my intuition and my ego. My intuition knew the truth. But my ego tried to trick me into believing otherwise. I was exhausted from the game and just wished it would end.

There are many times that I tried to convince myself to turn back. I hadn't come out to Chris. The friends and therapists I had come out to at that point, I could count on five fingers. I knew that even if they knew my truth, they would also understand if I came back with a "JK. Not gay" decision. Maybe. They knew what I was putting on the line by coming out. Surely, they saw the weight of what I had ahead of me and could see how it was slowly crushing me into the ground. They would understand if I decided I couldn't go any further and wanted to keep life as-is.

We all question ourselves and our actions, whether it's what to order at a restaurant, where to live, whether those shoes match that outfit, or whether we should come out as gay and end a nearly perfect relationship and everything that is known and comfortable in life. You know . . . daily decisions where we weigh out the benefits and consequences of our choices.

The potential consequence of losing the kids weighed heavily on me. I was entirely unfamiliar with family law. I also knew Chris had an incredibly supportive troop of Roman Catholic and Southern Baptist family members at the ready, armed with their faith and healthy bank accounts to pay lawyers. I had witnessed in previous years the gruesome custody battle over another young relative in the family and saw what lengths people would go to, prioritizing "winning" over the welfare of the child.

I believed that I was strong enough to accept other people's judgments about me being a lesbian. I knew I was not strong enough to risk losing my babies to lawyers. Whether I had blown the reality of that possibility out of proportion or not, I had nightmares about going in front of a homophobic judge who would ignore my parenting record, which included hundreds of hours of bedtime reading and the obvious loving bond that I shared with Sophie and Oliver. I knew that a lifetime's worth of solid character and good deeds could be wiped away in someone's mind the second that *lesbian* became an adjective to describe me. It might supersede everything.

So many times I came close to turning back. I had no "proof" I was gay, aside from the years of feeling gay, being attracted to women, and admitting to myself in therapy that I was gay. (Okay, maybe all of that *was* enough.) I had lived this long as a heterosexual and wondered why I couldn't just try and continue to do so for however long I needed. Maybe I could suck it up for another 12 years until both kids were in college. Then I could come out to minimize the impact on everyone. And Chris and I could start our lives over in our early 50s rather than our late 30s.

I will be eternally grateful to skilled therapists, life coaches, and wise friends who formed a safety net around me. They're the ones who, when you feel like your life is spinning out of control, grab the rusty metal bars and pull the merry-go-round to a stop before you fly off. I had nearly reached the point of letting centrifugal force do its thing and fling me all the way back into hetero-town, when I decided to finally seek the help of a life coach who could bring the spinning to a dead stop. "Picture your daughter, Sophie," she started.

I smiled as I envisioned my wildly creative, strongly opinionated, beautiful soul child. "Now imagine that Sophie is in the exact same position you are now. She knows a truth about herself that she has been hiding. She's not sure if other people will love or accept her, but she has been struggling with this internally for quite some time. It is starting to affect her physical and mental health. But she doesn't want to let you down. What would you want her to do?"

There wasn't even a moment of thought in my brain before the words shot forth from my mouth like a mama bear roar. "I would tell her to be herself!" I further punctuated the statement with a less-than-poetic, *"Duh!"* The life coach artfully paused, allowing me to marinate in the juices of my own self-realization.

As this truth took over my brain, my coach followed up with the clincher, "You are setting an example for Sophie, and she is watching you. If you wouldn't want her to hide an important part of herself, then don't teach her that this is good enough for you to do."

Life was reframed. I no longer viewed my coming out as a selfish or self-serving act. It was a lesson to my children to know and love who they are—all of the pieces, even the ones that society or others in their life might consider unlovable. It was also a gift of permission. My children had to know how to identify when things didn't feel right and know that they were allowed to course-correct, even if it meant flipping their world on its head.

What greater gift could I give them?

STAGE FOUR

THE PEAK OF PAIN

SECOND-BEST-CASE SCENARIO

While my path toward entering my identity became clear, the battle with my mind trolls raged on. A new war was initiated in my mind every time I looked at my children's freckled faces or into Chris's innocent blue eyes. Agnieszka knew my truth. Tisa knew my truth. Jack Daniel's knew my truth. But the circle was small, and Jack ended up being the one I turned to for support the most. Jack was my new nightly companion, poured over ice. It was never a lot, probably not even a full shot. I didn't want to get drunk. I just wanted to numb myself from the day. Take the edge off. Maybe help lull me to sleep.

I was aware that addictive behaviors existed within my extended family and was overly conscious of not falling into that. What I didn't know at that time was that drug and alcohol abuse were also a serious problem within the LGBTQ+ community. A 2016 report by the Substance Abuse and Mental Health Services Administration found that LGBTQ adults were almost twice as likely as heterosexual adults to have a substance abuse disorder with drugs or alcohol.[4] Factors like lack of support, discrimination, societal pressures, and internalized homophobia play a strong role in refilling the glass, popping the pill, or smoking the joint. I told myself that I didn't have a problem because I was controlling the small amount I drank. I didn't see the problem in craving and *needing* that small drink each night. For once, I was grateful for the perfectionist within me who kept me from denying myself the things I wanted in life—even alcohol.

The numbness from alcohol felt good after hours of constant overwhelm, but balancing stress and sedation can only exist for so long and it was starting to show. My eyes looked as if someone drew dark circles with a black Sharpie under them, like some drunken college prank. I was down more than 10 pounds, something that looked drastic on my already slight frame. My hair became brittle and began to clog the drain each time I showered. I started to menstruate every two weeks, and the lack of iron made me weaker than the insomnia. A poor diet, with caffeine and alcohol as the primary food groups, set my bowels on fire and they started to bleed as well.

One day the bleeding was so bad that I checked myself into urgent care. The nurse asked if I had ever had a colonoscopy or a family history of colon cancer. Her eyes looked concerned. I wasn't in the place to tell her that I knew the source of my downward health spiral. Instead, I promised her I'd follow up with a gastroenterologist.

The stress of staying closeted was no longer sustainable. With my declining health, I had to make a change or else nobody would get to have me: not Chris, not the kids, not a future partner. I went back to where the disintegration started, in my mental state, and sought out a trained professional who could help me fix it so that my body could begin to heal. Serendipity (and a well-timed

Facebook post) brought me to reconnect with an old friend of mine from years past.

Rachel was the sister of one of my closest friends. I knew Rachel was a qualified counselor and life coach. I also knew Rachel had been through a divorce with children and had even written a book, *Love Affair 101: The 5 Keys to Taking Charge of Your Life and Feeling Loved Again After Divorce.* Most importantly, I knew Rachel was a safe space for a closeted lesbian to share her truth. She was a known ally to the LGBTQ+ community and I could trust her.

Her megawatt smile and infectious laugh broke down my fear as I poured my emotional guts onto the floor over a Zoom call. She listened intently and with a warmth in her face that let my words flow easily. Then Rachel proposed a three-pronged plan called The Three Cs. It seemed overly simple: on the top of a page write the words *Comfort, Community,* and *Control.* Each word got its own page. She then instructed me to fill each page with the things or people that fit each of those descriptions. What brought me comfort and made me feel better on the hard days? Who did I have in my community that would be my social safety net over the coming years? What things in my life were in my realm of control?

Comfort was easy for me as I scrawled a long list of things like "my favorite mug filled with an endless flow of hot coffee or tea," "my fuzzy robe and weighted blanket," "hugs from my children that wrap around me like squid tentacles." I realized that most things that brought me comfort were already at my disposal and cost little to nothing. Reincorporating healthy choices that made me feel good was a step that I could definitely take. Rachel encouraged me to set a goal of partaking in at least three comfort items per day. I was happy to comply.

Community became a bit harder. While I had collected a broad network of friends and acquaintances across my lifetime, the depth of those connections was lacking. Add to it the additional fact that I didn't know who would be okay with my status as a lesbian and whose inner homophobia might come roaring out. I trusted that my close group of homeschooling mom friends would have my back. They were open-minded and supportive women who showed up for each other when times got tough. I also knew that I could include Agnieszka and several of my former coworkers from my massage school days on that list as well.

I flinched when I thought of my family members, though, carefully assessing each one to take an educated guess as to which side of the line they'd fall. For my own self-preservation, I left most of them off. It would hurt more to think they were my community and have them prove me wrong, than the other way around. Even without them, I managed to fill the Community page with names. It felt reassuring to know that there were people out there who would support me, even if just from the periphery. I suddenly felt less alone.

Control became the biggest lightbulb moment for me. My story in recent months had been that I was out of control, that I had taken my hands off the wheel and was now just bracing for impact. That was not an appropriate response for me to write on the page, though. Rachel gently reminded me that I could control my thoughts. I had control over my identity. I had control over many of my choices and decisions. I could control if Jack or water filled my glass at night. I could control whether I lost myself in Facebook or made it a daily goal to meditate. And while I couldn't control what everyone's reaction would be to me coming out, I could control my preparation for it. Taking back some control, in a time of so many unknowns, felt like a true gift.

Those three Cs illuminated how I would approach the fourth C . . . Chris. True, I could not predict his reaction, but I could envision multiple scenarios and have a plan for each. That alone brought me comfort.

My worst-case scenario was him completely losing his shit and flying into a rage, immediately kicking me out of our home and freezing our bank accounts. Although I found this scenario extremely unlikely, given his decades of sound mind and good character, I didn't want to ignore that my unexpected revelation might produce an unexpected result. I packed a "Go Bag" of clothes, a few toiletries, important paperwork, and a wad of cash. I asked Tisa if I could crash at her place for a few nights, should the need arise. She was my Community and would be there for me.

My best-case scenario was that Chris would reveal to me that he was gay also. I found this scenario even less likely than my worst-case scenario, but figured if I was going to brainstorm anything, then two gays would be better than one. For a fleeting moment, I envisioned us hanging at Pride picnics together while the kids frolicked through bubbles in rainbow attire. Perhaps it wasn't completely out of the realm of possibility, I hoped. Reality clapped back with the fact that this was highly unlikely given his attraction to me.

On to my second-best-case scenario and something slightly more probable. I envisioned he would show me compassion. He might even understand. I saw us working through this. Everything would be okay.

I'm not the praying type, but I prayed for this second-best-case scenario.

AFTER KNOWING

When the day came, I knew what was ahead. It didn't feel like a conscious choice to come out to my husband that day. My body and my emotions had decided for me. *Enough already!* they screamed as the toll of walking through life with this secret finally became too much. This was it.

I knew there wasn't a "going back" after this coming out to Chris, my first serious boyfriend and now husband—my partner for the past 19 years. Even if somehow we could figure out how to make it work, telling him I was a lesbian would forever change us. It was an unalterable shift. It would be that scar that's always there as a reminder of the injury, regardless of how well you've healed. Irrevocable.

Fear permeated each cell in my body as I drove to our craft beer bar to meet him that Wednesday. The bar didn't open until 3 P.M. that day and my mom was back at home playing with the kids so that Chris and I could have a meeting to discuss strategy and operations. He picked up sushi from the supermarket for our lunch.

My hands gripped the steering wheel tightly as I held a pep talk with myself that everything would be okay. He was a good human. We would get through this. We could set the example on how this could be done with grace and understanding. I am fortunate that my mind spared me from the mental overload of thinking through all the scenarios—the worst-case scenarios. I focused on the road and traffic around me as I tried not to puke or cry, or both.

As my car pulled into the parking lot behind the bar, I watched the trash cats scatter around the dumpster area. "Oh, to be a trash cat right now," I brooded. I grabbed my phone and opened the group text with Tisa and my other close friend Bree, who had been looped into the details of my life.

"This is it," I typed. "I'm telling him now. I can't wait any longer."

I didn't wait for a response as I turned off the ringer and shoved the phone into the back pocket of my jeans.

Fuck. Was this really my life?

Deep breath.

I walked into the back hallway of the bar and saw Chris in the main bar area up ahead, leaning over the countertop and unpacking our sushi.

Fuck.

I quickly turned left into our office without even muttering a hello. I couldn't speak if I tried. There was no air in my lungs. My mouth was parchment. The tears that I so carefully held back during my drive now flooded from my eyes in a heavy, constant stream. Giant, wet tears rained onto my shirt and the gray concrete floor. I started shaking.

I know Chris had been talking to me from the bar area during that time. I could hear words. I couldn't get a sound out to respond, though. In his concern, he walked back to the office and found me in my dissolving state. Big arms wrapped around me for a reassuring hug that I didn't feel I deserved. What I felt now, he would feel soon. That was a disgusting knowing to have.

He was clearly concerned. This was not me. He looked into my eyes for answers. "Babe, what's wrong? What's wrong? Talk to me. What happened?" His voice became more urgent and his eyes more pleading with each word.

I didn't know what to do. I tried moving my mouth over and over and still could not produce an audible sound. The pain of what I had to do made my skin crawl and I wrestled myself away from him to grab a heavy box of T-shirts. I pushed my way past him to the main bar area so that I would feel less claustrophobic. I needed air, like somehow it wasn't all around me. *Oxygen, oxygen everywhere, but not a drop to breathe,* I thought in an odd dalliance. My mind became desperate for a brief reprieve as I began the busywork of restocking merchandise shelves. He looked terrified. This was a Jill that neither of us recognized.

My hands shook violently as I tried to pick up a bar T-shirt and fold it neatly. I could have just as easily gotten a potbelly pig to sit on a barstool—both were fruitless and impossible tasks. He continued to dodge in front of me, bending his knees so our eyes were level. I swear that tears started to form in his as he looked at my face. He asked one last time, "What is it?"

I backed away slightly. "I'm . . . gay," I said as little bits of oxygen seemed to drop back into my lungs like sharply carved ice cubes. My head shook from side to side as I found my voice. "I'm so sorry. I'm so sorry," I whispered over and over again. A new wave of tears fell heavily against the cold floor. His hands rose up to both sides of his head and then clenched into fists just above his ears.

He took a few steps away from me. I quickly scanned the room for breakable glassware that might be within reach as he lumbered toward the front door, only to drop in a crouch with his hands holding his head. He was now a small ball on the floor—experiencing the same hollow-shell feeling I had just moments before. It was as if I had transferred the feeling to him. I suddenly felt an odd sense of calm. Not good. Not content. Just composed. That moment that had been haunting me for months had finally arrived. One of us was still standing. I was shocked and horrified that it was me.

Chris took a deep breath in, stood up, and came back my way with a facial expression that seemed to waver across the fine line of heartbreak, rage, desperation, and confusion. "What do you mean? Are you seeing someone? When did this happen?" Questions poured from him as he looked into my eyes for any answer that wouldn't affirm what I had just told him.

"There's nobody else. I just know and I couldn't keep it from you any longer. I've been walking around carrying this since I had CST this summer with Agnieszka. I can't do it anymore. I can't keep going on like this isn't the truth. It's killing me."

And then he responded in a way that will forever be etched in my mind as the permanent reminder of his quality of character. "That must have been really hard for you." He was superhuman in that moment. I had just hit him with the tidal wave he never saw coming and he returned that action with empathy. Understanding that what he was now feeling, I had been feeling on my own for months. This was my second-best-case scenario come true. At that point, I knew we would get through this.

We didn't have many more words in that moment. I looked toward the sushi and my stomach turned. I doubted I'd have an appetite for a long time. The security alarm on the door beeped as an older gentleman walked in through the front door. He had noticed that Chris's easily identifiable silver Scion decorated in beer stickers was parked out front. He thought it might be a good time to discuss his upcoming charity BBQ event. His timing could have only been worse had he arrived four minutes sooner.

Chris and I made eye contact one last time before I beelined to the back door to begin life after that moment. Of all the events that had come before and would come after, none were as significant as what had just occurred. It was the defining moment where all other memories would henceforth be sorted into "before knowing" and "after knowing."

I pulled out my phone and stared at the time. Forty minutes left until I had to return home to the kids. Forty minutes to pull myself together and hope that my eyes would be less swollen and my nose less blotchy and crimson. Forty minutes to pretend that what just happened didn't just happen, so that they could go on living peacefully unaware until Chris and I had a plan.

My lock screen showed I had messages waiting. They were of love, strength, and encouragement from Bree and Tisa. I fumbled for something funny or eloquent to write back and settled for a meager, "I did it."

Fuck.

Deep breath.

I started the ignition of my minivan and drove home to be mom and go on with life as usual.

WINNING LOTTO TICKETS AND WAVES

What do you do when you're a lesbian married to a straight man? I didn't know. There didn't seem to be a playbook, or if there was, I didn't even have the wherewithal to consider searching for it online. The weight of our new reality was crippling. For Chris and me, our "after knowing" life had begun.

Our relationship with each other was really all we had ever known. We were best friends. We enjoyed each other's company. We did a solid job raising children, running a business, and everything else we were supposed to do in life. Few people understand the type of pain that comes from ending a healthy marriage. My mind would always play back scenes of women telling me how lucky I was to have found such a kind, good-looking man. At our engagement party over a decade prior, my single aunt had asked me, "Does he have any available older brothers?" I wondered if I had been handed the winning lottery ticket of spouses and was turning it in, optimistically believing that somehow I had good enough odds to win again. I felt greedy and disgusting at times. There were even moments when I wished he had cheated on me or gambled away our income or done *something* to warrant this divorce. The perfectionist in me couldn't cope with the fact that I was the driving force behind our marriage ending. The mama bear in me cried in pain at the fact that my sexual orientation was causing the breakup of my children's stable home.

We both took a hiatus from work in those early weeks of the "after knowing," only performing the bare minimum needed to keep the bar afloat. Our days were filled with words and tears, tears and words. So many words. Chris and I joked that we spoke more in the week after me coming out than we had in our entire relationship of nearly two decades. I had always craved words from him. We were finally having the deep conversations I longed to have with him about feelings and our relationship, though never imagined I would get those conversations under these circumstances. The kids never questioned the overwhelming amount of screen time they had suddenly been granted. We processed our new reality while they built new worlds in Minecraft.

Like the five stages of grief, our conversations started in denial. Who said we had to get a divorce just because I was gay and he was straight? We *could* stay together if we wanted to—we would just need new ground rules. We talked through every option that might mean keeping our relationship and our lives intact. What if we had an open relationship, where we could fulfill our sexual desires on the side? What if we continued our relationship with a sexless marriage? We could join the ranks of couples who slept in separate beds. Despite my work as a massage therapist, I had never been a huge fan of touch or being touched. I remember reading the book *The Five Love Languages* by Gary Chapman and scoffing that "physical touch" was only the love language of men. Perhaps we could just remove the touch part from our otherwise solid existence. We considered bringing another woman into our relationship, however finding a unicorn is no easy task, and it didn't address the fact that I could no longer be intimate with him.

It was a hard pill to swallow when we realized that these options would serve us in the short term, but none of them would make things better in the long run because, at the end of the day, this didn't just come down to sex. I wanted a complete relationship and I wanted him to experience the same.

What seems to be a common misconception about the lesbian, gay, and bisexual community is that their identity boils down to who they like to have sex with. After all, if you've ever heard someone say, "What you do behind closed doors is none of my business," then you see what I mean about queer relationships being nothing more than what happens in the bedroom.

I wasn't looking for just sex. To me, being a lesbian was more than just the sum of the parts between my partner's legs. I wanted the experience of loving with my whole heart. I wanted to love without a wall that blocked me from trusting and letting go. I wanted the deep conversations with all the words . . . so many words every single day. I wanted all of the emotions, the vulnerability, the surrender, the nurturing. I wanted my mind set ablaze by a wildly witty and independent woman who defied the cultural norms of believing she had to be cared for by a man. I wanted the whole life, not just the sex.

And, while I don't know if he knew it yet, I hoped that he would realize how my sexual orientation had stunted the growth of our love. I wanted him to feel the level of love he had always shown me, but that I couldn't reciprocate. The truth is, in our current relationship, as good as it was, we were both missing out on the fullest expression of love. Chris and I had difficult and separate roads ahead with no guarantee that either of us would find another meaningful relationship in our lifetimes.

Knowing that our marriage would inevitably come to an end, our thoughts turned to the kids. We questioned if we should just wait 12 more years until Sophie and Oliver were grown and out of the house. I had already waited so long to come out and we had been able to maintain a bond throughout that time. What would it be to just wait one more decade? One. More. Decade.

The Universe stepped in and answered that question for us. On an unseasonably chilly Florida day, I had a fortuitous meeting with Denise, a fellow homeschooling mom who also served as the kids' tutor. She spent the beginning of the meeting rhapsodizing about how lovely Sophie and Oliver were, how creative, how funny. "They're really doing great here. They've made huge improvements in a short time," she shared. I liked her. She was an amazingly talented educator with a huge heart for her work.

She also knew that I had fallen off the homeschooling wagon, hit a rock, tumbled through the dirt, and gotten peed on by a desert lizard. If this was the Oregon Trail of homeschooling, I had died of dysentery long ago. In spite of that, she didn't make me feel like a total loser and shitty parent. She just extended her hand to help me back on track. In that moment, I decided to confess to her why homeschooling had been such an absolute struggle for me and how a divorce was looming in our family's future. I told her, "Sometimes I just feel so guilty knowing I am putting everyone's lives in such turmoil."

She knew just what to say. Instead of the half-genuine "kids are resilient" comment with a pat on my back, she shared a story of what her husband's own family was going through at that moment. He was now a grown adult. He was married and had several children. He just learned that after nearly 40 years of marriage, his parents were getting a divorce due to his father's repeated infidelity. In her late 60s, his mom could no longer take it. They were done.

Instead of the divorce being easier by waiting to deal with it until the kids were grown and out of the house, it sent the family into a tailspin, unwrapping questions and unraveling lies. Everyone wondered why they waited so long. They questioned how many times the father had repeated this behavior. They wondered why their mom allowed it for so long. Suddenly the memories of Denise's husband's youth were tainted with the new knowledge that the seemingly happy example of marriage that had been created was just a facade. And there was no chance to make new childhood memories anymore.

It was a hard pill for me to swallow, realizing that causing pain to our family was inevitable. We could let the tidal wave of divorce hit our family now, or let the wave hit our family later. It was going to hit us either way, and when it did it would hurt. Chris and I put on our metaphorical goggles and wet suits and trudged forward into the next phase.

ARE YOU SURE?

Processing the end of our relationship was a tough time for both of us. However, I was unprepared for the additional load that came with figuring out and understanding my new identity and sexuality. I had been so focused on the external changes of my life, that for a while I missed the internal transformations taking place in my mind and body to help cope with the massive upheaval around me. Rather than intellectualize and analyze further, I would mentally collapse into what felt like just the workings of my primitive brain. You know, the reptilian one that is all about survival and eating bugs. However, this time I was the bug. A mosquito, actually. And a blue light from my past glowed back into view.

I wish I had known that there can be a period in the coming-out process known as "delayed adolescence" or "second adolescence." Coming across the mention of it in an episode of *Queer Eye* was a lightbulb moment for me. Delayed adolescence seems to happen when people come out later in life and regress back to a period in time, usually their teenage years, when they first started denying themselves their truth.

My whims and emotions were all over the place. I wanted tattoos and started a Pinterest board of the most badass ink I could find (because Pinterest is how white, suburban moms do badass). I dreamed of shaving part of my head and coloring my hair in a wild rainbow of hues. I polled Facebook as to whether or not I should get my nose pierced. I bought faux leather pants off Amazon for $20 . . . and actually wore them out in public with my Converse sneakers. A friend told me I looked like the middle-aged Avril Lavigne.

When I was with my family, I used every stitch of strength I had to hold myself together and maintain the status quo. On my own time or with friends, however, I started to live the teenage years that I had never experienced before. I was wild. I was rebellious. A friend, without knowing the reasons why, commented to me that I seemed to have a new "to hell with it all" attitude. She was right. Like a moody teen, my prefrontal cortex seemed underdeveloped. My reptilian brain was in charge now.

Everything in my life became more extreme. I partied hard. Cried harder. Fought hard to be a good parent and not expose my kids and Chris to what my insides were feeling. Fought harder on the tae kwon do mat, where sparring opponents and heavy bags could absorb my phrenic energy. I was wild, but not in the untamed cheetah way that Glennon Doyle would eventually empower us to be. I felt like a rabid, starving creature willing to accept whatever was offered to me to make the hunger pain subside. I didn't care what came my way. I just wanted to be fed.

My immaturity had injured me in the martial arts ring. I took on an opponent who outweighed and outskilled me in so many ways, that I walked away with a painful shoulder injury. Although I felt like a teen, my body no longer recovered like one. This injury I couldn't shake off and I knew I would need therapeutic help to recover. It was time to reconnect with one of the most intuitive and talented massage therapists I knew. I called Amy and set up an appointment.

Amy melded her hands onto my bare back, palpating the damage and formulating a treatment plan. I lay there like a sad puppy, embarrassed that I hurt myself trying to prove my fighting skills, while also hoping that the conversation wouldn't steer its way into *why* I suddenly felt the need to take out so much rage. *Just keep asking about her,* I told myself.

Amy shared that she was fresh off another breakup from her fiancée, still licking the wounds of what their life together could have been. I found myself acting just like I did during our old beach days a decade prior. I hung on her every word, offering encouragement that this hurt would pass and she was on a healthier road ahead. Our discussion was limited, though. We were both wading in the superficial conversation waters. Deep diving into feelings was not her favorite pastime and not where I had any interest in going at that moment.

"So what the hell's up with you?" she twanged. I marveled at the fact that a decade of living in Florida had only barely dulled her Georgian accent. Dang it! She was done talking and now it was my turn. I am a pretty terrible liar with zero poker face. Fortunately for me, my face was buried into the fabric cover of the massage table's face cradle. I bit my upper lip and stared at the floor praying that anything but the obvious, glaring situation would pop into my head. Could I talk about work? No. I was barely doing anything for the bar and had nothing noteworthy to share. Could I talk about the kids? And what? Share their latest video game win?

My brain felt on fire, torturing me into sharing the intimate details of my life revelation. *It would feel good to let another person know,* it told me. *If anyone will understand, it's her. She's one of you!* it said. Why did it feel so wrong to me? Maybe because I was scared that it could lead me down a conversational road that I was not ready to take. I inhaled deeply into my chest. Time to deep dive.

"I'm . . ." the word caught in my throat. I was so new to coming out to people and I wondered if it ever got easier. I choked out the word *gay* and finished with a massive exhale. I took a momentary pause to recover and then slowly lifted my eyes from the face cradle to see if she had heard what I just said. I couldn't quite crane my neck enough to make eye contact. Perhaps she was avoiding looking back at me.

"Are you sure?" she responded as more of an exclamation than a question. The tone of surprise in her voice caught me off guard. Like an old film projector that quickly skipped through frame after frame, my mind recapped our times together at the gay bars, gay beaches, and her softball games. She was a lesbian who had been with me at lesbian things, and she didn't think I could be a lesbian?

I felt like someone hit the kill switch in my soul. My mind expected joy and support. Instead, I got a question. *The* question. The one that burrowed in my brain and played on loop over and over. Are you sure? Am I sure? My newfound confidence in my identity exited my body in the form of tears. Her question brought up the greatest fear that I had spent little time exploring. What if I had done all of this, come out to Chris, created this irrevocable shift, and I was wrong?

I've learned that it's not uncommon when someone comes out later in life to have this push and pull between wondering if their sexual orientation is true. I knew what turned me on. I knew what I fantasized about. I knew the kind of relationship and love that I had always dreamed of feeling. I also knew what kind of touch felt unnatural and uncomfortable to me, as much as I tried to make myself okay with it. But the one thing I didn't know, the one question I hadn't been able to answer up until that point, was if I truly would be okay having an intimate sexual relationship with a woman. My body thought so. My mind maintained a shred of doubt that I could be wrong about it all and I could have just blown up my life over a nonfeeling.

I paused my internal struggle to respond to Amy, my insecurity pouring out of my mouth. "I mean, yeah. I think so. I haven't been with a woman but . . ."

She cut me off. "Well, there's only one way to find out." Then she let out a deep, guttural laugh. I didn't have words to respond. I couldn't tell if this was an actual invitation or just a joke. Was she expressing an interest in me or just encouraging me to shoot my shot in the wild world of Tampa Bay lesbians? I don't remember us talking much after that point. I lay there on the table, instead focusing on the physical pain of the trigger points to distract me from the mental pain of questioning my life.

Once my shoulder was on its way to repair and I was fully dressed, she took a seat on her couch to continue our conversation. My eyes were still glassy from crying and my nose was undoubtedly red as well. Aside from massage, she and I had never shared any other form of physical touch. While I'd like to pretend it was a moment of bravery, it was actually a moment of feeling so broken that there was no ego left to protect me. I asked Amy if I could sit next to her.

She put her arm on the back of the couch like a half-hug and I awkwardly sat down, slowly inching my way backward into the nook of her arm until our torsos and legs touched. I melted into her, feeling her softness. It was a different quality of touch than I was used to. It was awkward and foreign at first, but I didn't want it to stop. My memory flashed back to holding another girl's hand in Bolivia. It was that same feeling again, but this time I understood why.

In that moment, I realized how badly I needed to be comforted and held. I realized that perhaps the hardest part of coming out to oneself is that for so long you do it alone. Your struggles, fears, pains, shame, and hardship are yours to bear. For those who come out to themselves while in a relationship with someone of another gender, you realize that the person you used to seek refuge in, your safe harbor, is now unavailable to you to process this knowing. In that moment, I just appreciated her hug.

NOT BROKEN

I took my familiar perch on the kitchen countertop, cradling a Cuban espresso in the hand of my newly fixed shoulder. Chris kept his distance with his own tiny espresso curled in his big hands like a delicate bird's nest. It was time for more words. I hoped he was ready to have the conversation I needed to have this time. After coming out to him at the bar, this was the next hardest thing to admit. I didn't want to cause more hurt. But I didn't know how to start healing without it.

"I wish I had a way to confirm that I am a lesbian." I regretted my wording. I didn't want it to seem like I was questioning, not to him nor to myself. "I mean, I know that I am," I continued. "I just wish . . . I just need to know that my body actually works. There is still a part of me that thinks maybe I'm just broken."

I thought I saw a glimmer of hope in Chris's eyes at those words. He seemed to glaze over the fact that I was seeking permission to have sex with a woman, instead focusing on the fact that if there was a possibility that I was broken then we could still be together. Perhaps a woman couldn't fix the situation. There was a microsliver of a chance that this wasn't the end for us. I don't know which outcome was better: broken but together or whole but divorced.

"It's too bad you don't have anyone to help you confirm that," he responded.

Before I could ponder if he even meant it, I smirked like a bashful teenager.

"Do you?" he asked with surprise.

The bubbles started to build inside of me. It was the feeling of excitement that we were having this conversation, tempered by the realization of how crushing such a conversation may be to him. I warned myself to proceed with caution.

"Well, I don't know if she really meant anything by it, but when I saw Amy the other day, I came out to her, and she joked about helping me find out."

I tried to read his eyes, while also wishing to curl up like a potato bug and roll away into a hole for even suggesting such a thing. This was a hard part of the process, wanting to be honest with him now but also wanting to spare his feelings. How could I confirm I was a lesbian, so we could both move forward, without destroying him? But if I couldn't confirm things, would we ever be able to move forward or would we stay stuck in questioning purgatory?

"I'm sorry. But I do wonder if she . . . if that's what . . . maybe I can . . ." I stammered for the right way to tell my husband that I was interested in having sexual intercourse with my longtime friend. I realized it was not a conversation that I felt adequately or eloquently prepared for. In the moment, I just tried to balance emotional damage control with those resurfacing feelings of excitement that I had had back when she and I had gone to the gay bars. It was like walking across verbal eggshells while wearing a heavy pair of Doc Martens.

"Why don't you see if she's up for it," he said. His comment surprised us both. Inside he wilted. Inside I bloomed.

I knew Amy was off work. I knew the kids had an afternoon of play planned with my mom. I typed on my phone, "Can I come over?" but couldn't hit the send button. Was I really ready for this? Another big step on the rainbow road?

"Universe," I said with my eyes skyward, "send me a sign." Billie Eilish's song "Bad Guy" started on the radio. Sign? I don't know, but it was enough for me. It felt wrong. I felt bad. And now my theme song was playing.

"Fuck it!" I said, hitting the send button. I hopped in my car and began the half-hour drive to her house, hoping that she would reply back sometime before the 29-minute mark with a "Yeah!" She did. Game on. I didn't know what I was about to get into, but I hoped it was going to involve lesbianing like lesbians. I was about to become one of them. Out in the wild. My rabid carcass growled.

I pulled my minivan into her driveway and gave myself one last look in the mirror. Perhaps this would be the last time I would see myself this way. There was about to be another irrevocable shift. I would enter with one identity and leave with another. I exhaled, swore one more time, and walked through her front door.

"So, what are you here for?" Amy asked, partially questioning and partially waiting for me to just confirm what she already suspected. I could barely speak. "You know how you mentioned a threesome?" I said. "What about just two?" I wasn't sure if my line came out as corny or seductive. At that point, I no longer cared. My body was on fire. I was ready to let my past self burn.

She ushered me into her bedroom and motioned for me to sit on the bed. "Jill," she said slowly and deliberately, "I need you to tell me what you want." Now there seemed to be a bit of concern. Perhaps she knew that this moment would end up being a definitive one for me as well. I knew she had already been "the first" for other questioning women. While my mind could only envision positive outcomes for whatever lay ahead, I imagined that she had seen other scenarios as well.

I couldn't say words. Not out loud. I smiled. I blushed. She pushed again, "What are you looking to do?" her eyes large and pleading for some form of clarification. I put a hand on her waist and leaned in close to her, not sure of what to do next. I hoped my physical cues would help where my words failed and that she would make the next move. She took the bait.

I felt her soft lips and smooth skin press firmly against mine. I pulled away slightly and we locked eyes. There was no more verbal communication needed. She saw my hunger. My growl turned to a roar.

Things escalated quickly. I had waited to be intimate with a woman for so long that the thought of prolonging things even a minute more, taking time for buildup, seemed unbearable. I was reckless. I was in full teenage mode, sopping with desperation and urgency in my touch. She asked me not to touch her. She wasn't comfortable with anyone touching her. Not in that way, at least.

My role was to relinquish my power and give her full control. I was more than happy to do so. It felt so good to not be in charge. To just give in fully and let someone else make the decisions. She was confident and direct. Time paused and I took a moment to relish how delicious it felt to be touched and to *want* to be touched. Despite all the excitement and nerves, my body was relaxed and inviting. My previous intimacy barriers of "not there" or "not like that" were gone.

For the first time in my life, sex felt natural. I laughed to myself at that thought. So many years of my life I had heard people say how unnatural same-sex relationships were, completely disregarding that they exist in over 1,500 animal species. And here I was now, with a woman and feeling like it was where my body was always supposed to be, doing what it was always supposed to do. My body knew. This was my nature.

That experience with Amy opened many new pathways in my mind. I was not broken. My body worked as intended. I was grateful for the opportunity to confirm my sexual identity. Amy was a best-case scenario in my coming-out process. She was experienced and talented, willing to be a teacher and not criticize or embarrass me for my mistakes or desperation. Being with her was like becoming a lesbian with training wheels on. It took a long time for my high to wear off that day.

But time passed and now I had a new problem. I understood why some people went crazy for sex. Sex was like a drug, my feel-good to escape the pain that consumed every other aspect of my life. The days between the next time I was available and when Amy was interested in having me over seemed to drag by. My mind was consumed with replaying every moment of our encounters, trying to recall each scent and sensation. Netflix movies would no longer suffice. My body was desperate for the next hit.

Amy wasn't on the same page. She was happy to oblige my urges when she felt lonely or wanted a solid snuggle, but she wanted nothing beyond that. I tried to convince myself that Amy would come around eventually. She'd realize that I was a catch. She'd see that, although we were total opposites in every way and wanted completely different things out of life, we could figure things out. We didn't have to be alone. I didn't have to be alone.

And also, I wasn't alone. Chris and I still lived under the same roof, albeit in different bedrooms. He was beginning to explore dating too and quickly realized what had been missing from our relationship. The chasm between us was growing wider by the day. We both knew that any chance for maintaining a life together was officially over. We could only move forward, at best, as friends. While taking our time seemed to be a gift, it also meant going through our challenging process privately. We thought it best to keep things under wraps from our kids and family. It wasn't the right time. It would have been too much change at once. And the holiday season was coming.

FAKING IT AND FAMILY PHOTOS

The roof of our home was like the butterfly bandage that just barely kept the wounded relationship between Chris and me from splitting wide open. The kids were starting to notice, peppering us with questions about why Mom and Dad were no longer sleeping in the same room. We blamed it on his late-night bar schedule and my need for a solid night of rest to homeschool, work, and parent each day. It was a painful time for Chris and me both now, trying to live this double life: maintain an appearance of family to everyone else, while exploring what life apart felt like. Our days were filled with emotional highs and lows like we had never experienced before in our relationship. We used to be so even keel.

In some ways, going through our own individual traumas together, Chris and I were becoming closer. This surprised us both, actually. Our conversations now were more honest and direct than they had ever been. In the past, we let things roll to keep the peace. Now we just wanted realness and someone we could vent to and process with. We had clarity on what that missing piece was and why we had never fit together quite right, like two puzzle pieces that you try to force together because they look like they're a match, but they're not for some small reason. I could see the pain on his face, though, any time he asked a question about Amy. Did I enjoy my time with her? Is this what I really wanted? His sparks of hope were extinguished every time he asked. At least it removed the uncertainty of where we were headed.

United in this front, we decided that the best course of action would be to wait until January or February to begin sharing news of our divorce, and our shocking reason why, with family and our children. We'd let Thanksgiving and Christmas pass without issue. We'd even potentially get through the kids' January birthdays without any stress or struggle. When life felt like chaos, this was our little way of taking back control. We recognized that we had the power of choice and could do things on our terms.

Thanksgiving was here before we knew it, and it was our year to celebrate with his parents and siblings. We loaded the kids into the minivan to head south to Chris's sister's apartment where everyone would convene. We had one queen-sized bed for our family of four to sleep in. He found somewhere else in the apartment to crash. Using the excuse that the kids wanted to snuggle me in bed was a highly plausible half-truth to tell his family.

The kids were excited for holiday festivities and the unhealthy amounts of sugar they would soon be consuming. Chris and I were excited to have a diversion from our daily struggle. Our epically long conversations ceased completely once we were surrounded by others' ears. Instead, he shared updates on the bar with his parents and how it kept growing and getting better month by the month. He hoped for big things and possibly a second location in the year ahead . . . 2020. (Sigh. 2020 would indeed prove *not* to be the year for bar businesses to flourish.)

This was the year that Chris's sister had a big surprise to share. She quietly announced to Chris and me that she had arranged for a photographer to meet up with everyone the next day for a family photo session. This is something Chris's mom had wanted for years, and it was happening. Now. Of all years. (Double sigh.)

It didn't take long before my already taxed nervous system jumped into panic mode. I tried valiantly to keep my armpits from leaking onto my clothes so that I could maintain the appearance of calm from the outside. But my insides knew that I was about to ruin the family photo session that they had been waiting for. By the time these images were edited and printed, Chris and I would be close to our own big reveal that the woman in the photograph was probably their worst nightmare—a closet lesbian. I would render their photos obsolete, a painful reminder of the horrible person who blew up their dear, innocent son's life.

But silver linings come to us in the most bizarre of ways. I suddenly had a solution, thanks to my brain flashing back to the last time we had a family photo session: the day Chris and I got married. I remembered standing there in my long, white dress and train with faux buttons all the way down my back. Standing at the altar of the Catholic church with his family, the photographer snapped away until the moment my brand-new mother-in-law asked the photographer a favor. She told him she wanted a few photos with "just the family." I suddenly felt stares of shock and apology coming from the photographer, his assistant, and my bridal party, and we realized that this was code for me to step aside. And so, while my friends stood there looking aghast, I picked up my long gown and walked off to the periphery as I watched the photographer take pictures of my new family, without me in them. The discomfort of that moment, the embarrassment that I felt, would now become my saving grace. I could do this again, except I would have to be the one to suggest they get some "family shots" with everyone but me in them. Nearly a decade later, I wondered if anyone would fight it. I suspected nobody would. I let Chris know of my plan.

After dragging a comb through my daughter's waist-long hair and trying to get my son's hair not to resemble that of a baby duck's in a wind tunnel, everyone made their way to a local park for the photo session. Chris's nerves were palpable, as I'm sure mine were too. We shot nervous glances at each other, wondering if my scheme to position myself on the periphery of nearly every shot and to hop out of frame would work.

Anytime I suggested, "Why don't you get a shot of just the 'core family'? Why not the 'core family' plus the kids?" nobody questioned it, particularly when Chris would chime in with, "Oh yeah! What a great idea." I couldn't tell if anyone cared that I was the one and only person not in the pictures. I tried to fade into the surrounding banyan trees off on the sidelines, hoping that nobody would remember I was there and ask me to rejoin the pictures. Nobody did. They already knew my puzzle piece didn't quite fit with theirs, without knowing the reason why.

By the time Christmas rolled around, we felt more comfortable being able to successfully navigate time with his family without letting on about our personal struggles.

This time we would road trip up to South Carolina to stay with Chris's aunt and uncle. The entire extended family would convene in their home, which more closely resembled a bed and breakfast than a house for a retired couple. In spite of the layer of doom that now blanketed Chris and me, I was excited to see them both. His aunt, who we called Nana, had been the one person in his family who had always welcomed me as one of their own. We shared many cups of coffee and sweet tea in rocking chairs and around kitchen tables as she told me about her life, her grandbabies, her church, her friends, and her health. She was my ally in a group that didn't always seem to know what to make of me. She was also a Southern Baptist and could occasionally be overheard making a comment like "burn the witches" if we drove past a home with a rainbow flag. She was a paradox of God's love and the church's teachings.

Our Christmas visit passed uneventfully, just as Chris and I had hoped. Everyone overate, the kids were overgifted, and he and I were able to keep our emotional shit together through it all. To everyone else, we looked like life as usual. Our lack of public displays of affection was in step with years of absent public displays of affection. The growing distance between us was not perceptible to them. A true Christmas miracle.

As our van pulled away from Nana's house that final time, with his aunt and uncle standing on the porch waving at us as we honked the horn repeatedly to set off home, I cracked and the tears poured out of me uncontrollably. Within seconds I was a sobbing red mess. "What's wrong?" Chris asked with concern. "I'm just sad to leave. That was a really nice Christmas," I responded, realizing the kids were homing in on my sudden emotional moment. I couldn't say any more. But in that moment, it had dawned on me that I was setting eyes on Nana and his uncle for the last time. After that moment, as we pulled out of their neighborhood, I would most likely never be welcomed back for a cup of coffee or a sweet tea in a rocking chair again. Another irrevocable shift was coming.

STAGE FIVE

THE SLOW REBUILD

THE ELEPHANT CIRCLE

There's nothing like dressing up in Christmas pajamas and artistically flipping designs on a magic sequin pillow of Nicholas Cage's face. (Yes, that's really a thing.) Before the holiday season was done, we made sure to fit in our annual homeschooling moms' Christmas party. Janel threw the best parties for our group. The room was always festively decorated in a style somewhere between simplistic Scandinavian, with clean lines and warm whites, and sensory-pleasing Pottery Barn, with rugs that were oh-so-soft to touch and shed on you like you had just wrestled a Samoan dog. The music was a combination of '90s throwbacks and current pop songs. And she always had some new, fun cocktails mixed up for the occasion.

Perhaps what I liked most about the parties, though, is that they were what I pictured my teenage year having been like . . . if I had been a normal teen and hung out with friends instead of my mom. The benefit now was that I had my own set of wheels, no curfew, and a healthy dose of that "I don't give a fuck" attitude that slowly comes with age.

We were several drinks and a solid earful of Salt-N-Pepa in when we decided to begin the games. Seven of us ladies took a seat on the white shag rug. This group had named itself "The Twisted Roosters" after a pretzel-like yoga pose we all had attempted at our homeschooling co-op's yoga class. That wasn't the name of the pose. We had forgotten the name of the pose.

Another homeschooling mom, Jenny, halted the start of any activities to pass out small drawstring bags with "The Festive Farm Co." on them. Inside was a steel cut-out of an elephant with a hemp string to hang it as an ornament. I racked my brain to figure out the connection. Did elephants have something to do with roosters? Did Jenny go on safari this year and I completely forgot? Upon further digging, we found a note that accompanied the ornament.

"In the wild, female elephants are known as fierce protectors. They literally form a circle around sisters who are hurting or grieving. And often, they will kick dirt up around her to mask the scent of suffering . . . in turn, keeping her safe from predators.

"And yet, we are the same. This is what we do. This is who we are. And this is who we are meant to be for each other. We all have elephants in our lives. Sometimes we are the ones in the middle, and sometimes we're on the outside kicking up dirt with fierce, fierce love. But the circle remains."

Sweet sentiment. Thoughtful gift. We hugged. We commented about how awesome it was to have our group of friends. And then we moved on to drinking games and Truth or Dare.

I am a panicky Truth or Dare player to begin with. Both Truth and Dare seemed like precarious options for me to pick, given my current state of emergence from the closet. Tisa was the only one in the crowd who knew my recently acknowledged truth.

When it was my turn, the fear of having to kiss a dog on the lips or do anything involving boogers made me opt for Truth. In hindsight, what the actual fuck was I thinking?! But in the moment, I thought, *How bad could it be?* The answer is bad if you have a deep, dark secret and no poker face. Someone asked me a question about attraction to the husbands of the group. My snarky brain was ready to fire out, "Ha! I'm barely attracted to my own husband," when I realized that maybe that wasn't the most appropriate response or method to "come out" to the group. Instead, I froze. Literal deer in the headlights, with my eyes as large as Ping-Pong balls. I shot a glance to Tisa. She was shooting the same concerned glance to me. Fortunately, her mouth moved and she got out, "Inappropriate question. Nobody should answer that. Let's move on."

Phew! Safe from that one.

Eventually it was Jenny's turn and, as per the usual with her, someone asked a question about her being with women. While Jenny was happily married to a man and had two children, she had spent a good part of her 20s living the lesbian life before deciding that it wasn't how she pictured her future. Still, there seemed to be great curiosity in the group about what it was like to have an intimate relationship with another woman. And Jenny was a wonderfully open book on the subject of sexuality. Nothing was taboo for her, and I had always appreciated her candor and honesty.

And then she said it. "Am I the only one of this group that's ever been with a woman?" Panic again. I froze and just barely thawed my eyeballs enough to shoot a terrified glance to Tisa, who seemed to be shooting a "you don't have to say anything yet" glance my way. Jenny must have caught wind of our exchange, or the fact that I was probably beet red, or that I may have awkwardly also puffed out my cheeks like a puffer fish in an attempt to protect myself.

"You too?" She said with a surprised grin. Five other sets of eyes whipped around in my direction. Tisa casually shook her head with a tiny "no" to remind me that I was under no obligation to share that I had come out to my husband a few months prior and was now fooling around with an old friend. It was too late. My brain had now decided that the only course of action was to tell them and hope for the best.

And so I did.

Once again, I have total amnesia related to this part of the night. Did I say the word *gay* or *lesbian*? No clue. I don't know what I told them or how I told them, but suddenly they all knew. And then they were all smiling and giving me supportive hugs and offering to help in whatever way I needed.

This was my first big coming out to a group. While I knew they loved me as a friend, and while they all knew Jenny was a retired lesbian, I still had fear that maybe some of them wouldn't be okay with it. Or they would question why I waited so long. Or they would question how this might hurt my kids. They didn't. There was nothing but encouragement and protection that night.

I knew where I was in the elephant circle, and I was grateful to know that I would have their safety ring around me in the coming months.

TWIN FLAMES

"Seven . . . six . . . five . . ." we counted down in unison as a large sequin-covered fish was lowered slowly on a rope pulley to ring in the new year. I stood there, filled with excitement and anticipation. It was my first time going out as a newly "out" person. I came with a date—a female date! We were at a gay bar, and I was surrounded by my new community that I hoped I could seamlessly slip into without anyone noticing. (They probably noticed. I was the only person that I saw, besides the drag queens, in high heels that night.)

"Three . . . two . . . one . . ." I averted my gaze from the disco fish, preparing for a serious kiss with my date for the night, Amy. And there she was, just a few steps away, in a full-on, face-sucking, body-groping make-out session with another woman. I wondered if anyone else heard the sound of my heart shattering on the floor over the crowd's cheers and celebratory noisemakers.

I knew we weren't exclusive. I knew she was seeing other people. I knew, the moment she started acting hypervigilant at the bar, that perhaps one of her other objects of interest was there that night. The lesbian pool, even in queer-friendly Tampa Bay, is not all that large, and the odds of running into someone you know are always in your favor. I knew Amy had a reputation for following her impulses over her better judgment. It was part of her intrigue and gave her that bad-girl vibe that made others abandon their sensibilities for a chance with her.

I was one of those women. I wanted to believe that we were different. We weren't. In that midnight moment, I felt as hollow and gutted as that fancy sequined fish.

Some gentle hands rested on my shoulders from behind me. I could feel the pity running through their veins. I turned around to see the faces of some new friends I had met that evening. They gave me a "sorry gal, that sucks" expression as they pulled me in for a hug and wished me a Happy New Year. They politely made awkward conversation with me to keep me distracted as I used every shred of willpower to hold myself together.

Ouch. This was a rough start to lesbian life.

Amy wasn't my catalyst—the person who made me realize I was a lesbian. A catalyst is typically the person who not only causes an attraction but also leads the person to seek a relationship. Your catalyst will take things beyond just attraction and propel you into action. In catalyst relationships, the highs can feel so incredibly high, and the lows can take you to new depths you may have never felt before. Sometimes catalyst relationships work out. Oftentimes they do not.

I had never sought a relationship with Amy in all our years of friendship. However, fresh out of the gay gate and bound for divorce from Chris, I was anxious to explore this new world that was now accessible to me. I was also terrified. I didn't know how to date when it came to hetero relationships and felt like a complete glitter fish out of water when it came to same-sex relationships. I had no idea where to start. I tried low-key searching on Facebook, joining local-area lesbian groups and hoping that someone would post "I'm single and patient and kind and am willing to teach a baby gay." I asked some dear lesbian friends of mine how I should go about finding someone. "You'll just meet people at the everyday activities you do," they responded. I'm not sure that they knew that the odds of me meeting a single lesbian at a homeschool park meetup were only slightly better than the odds of finding an available queer at a Catholic marriage retreat.

The fact that Amy was newly single and I was newly out around the same time seemed like serendipity. We already had a foundation of friendship and a level of trust with each other, and here we were, both hurting from loneliness at the same time. Initially she fulfilled a need in me that would have been difficult to fill with anyone else. She helped me confirm my sexual orientation and clear up the lingering doubts in my mind that maybe I was confused about my identity. Having that knowledge gave me the courage to move forward in the direction of my new life, trusting that my feelings were not just a midlife whim.

And I was like a constant stream of affirming memes in her life. When she would feel down, unloved, or need a "you are awesome" pep talk, I was there to nurture her with my words and hugs. She rarely let her tough exterior crack, but with me it seemed like she could let down her guard and know that she'd be safe. I could see that there was goodness at her core—and that's when I started to fall for her, knowing that she was not falling for me. I hoped that with just a few more encouraging words, maybe she would. She adamantly refused to label me as anything other than a friend. "Girlfriend" was never a title I would hold with her. Even still, I would look around her house and wonder if she'd let me change up some of the paint colors if I moved in. My mind created future hopes for our nonexistent relationship.

And this is why, in our short period of not-dating, we went through approximately 57 not-breakups. Every time I pushed to get close to her, she ran further away. Every time I built up our relationship in my mind, the truth of our situation would bring my heart crashing down. I started to realize that I was in love with the imaginary connection I had built in my mind, the highlight reel of our moments together with some creative made-up fantasies and romantic lines added in. And then when we were together, I would find myself utterly disappointed in our reality. The Amy of my mind I loved and wanted a future with. The Amy I was with left me feeling empty and frustrated. We were just Band-Aids to each other, trying to heal our own hurt. But every time we called it quits, the Band-Aid was ripped off and my wound grew larger.

I had told myself that I would not put myself through the agony of getting hurt again. *Love yourself, Jill. Know your worth, Jill. This is not what love feels like, Jill. You know better, Jill.*

But when New Year's Eve rolled around and I found myself in pain again, all my self-love talk dissolved like warm Jell-O as my scared-to-be-alone-forever talk kicked in. I texted my Band-Aid for another date and she accepted. That was our routine. My foolish ego wondered if maybe tonight she would see my worth. Maybe this new year would spark a feeling in her and we could start January with a fresh set of feelings for each other. (Do you remember when I said I was an eternal optimist? This is one way it bites me in the ass). As you know, our magical night didn't turn out that way, and I was hurt more deeply than ever before. That was it. I vowed to cut her out of my life.

But guess what?

That's not what baby gays do. In the middle of my mess and drama, I had reached a new self-esteem low. It took only three short weeks before I was back to negotiating with myself that maybe she had changed. Maybe she had learned her lesson. This time would be different. Right?

Stop shaking your head at me, reader.

This time, though, I knew I needed outside perspective. I had already burned out Tisa, Bree, and the rest of my overly patient friends with my roller-coaster ride of emotions for Amy. I was even starting to exhaust myself, with my ego, my rational mind, and my heart all duking it out daily to determine what role she had in my life. One part of me still held out hope for a relationship, if she could just turn a corner and be different than who she was. One part knew that I had violated our treaty by developing feelings in the first place. She had been clear from the beginning that she didn't want a relationship and I conveniently ignored that. And one part called her a no-good rotten scoundrel for treating me like a piece of flaming trash in the dumpster fire that was us.

I did what any rational person would do. I consulted a mystic.

Kerin Monaco, owner of the Wild-Hearted Collective on Facebook, was an astrologist and intuitive card reader who had recently entered my world. I didn't know much about tarot and oracle cards. I didn't know anything about mystics. But I liked her energy and found myself in awe of the guidance she had dropped on me in the past. I hoped that she could bring me some perspective on my situation as she connected with spirit guides. If a higher power didn't know, then who would?

"Why is this woman in my life?" I pleaded. "Am I supposed to be cutting her out, or is she the one I'm destined for?" I asked, as a piece of me held hope for the latter answer and prayed that Kerin wouldn't say the former.

"I'm picking up a strong twin-flame energy here," she replied. I had no idea what that meant. I hoped that if I Googled it, I'd find a definition describing it as a "hot and steamy soulmate experience." Nope. Not it. I told my teenage brain to simmer down.

Kerin explained that twin flames do not have to be a love interest but sometimes can be. More often they are a person in your life who shows you a side of yourself or teaches you a lesson that you may not have learned on your own. Twin flames bring about changes in each other in a way that other people cannot. They can be like the fast track to where you want to be in life, but the road is typically not smooth.

Kerin described my relationship with Amy as an uphill climb—a mountain, actually, not some moderate-level hiker's trail. It was not to say that we couldn't try to continue on this path, but it would not be easy and there would be many points of struggle. To make matters worse, our starting points for the climb were completely different. She encouraged me to look at what Amy brought out in me and what I potentially brought out in her.

It was a cosmic lightbulb moment. I got it now. Both my lust and anger for Amy subsided. I understood our purpose and saw that the emotional gauntlet I went through with her was an important part of my own self-discovery.

Amy showed me a different way of living. I had admired her from our massage school days for being brave enough to live openly as a lesbian woman. She wasn't just out, she was proud. I wanted to be too. I wondered if I would have ever figured myself out if I hadn't had her as an example. She helped me confirm my identity during a time when I considered turning back and recloseting myself. Without her, perhaps I would not have had the courage to explore who I truly was. I knew that moving forward I would have more confidence to start dating, now that everything wasn't so new to me.

Most importantly, she made me reexamine myself and who I was becoming. This was an important pivot point in my life, one where I had to decide the course of my future. I had found self-love, but my self-worth was seriously lacking. If I wanted good things in my life, I would have to start treating myself like I was worthy of them. If I accepted scraps, I would stay in that dumpster. Amy forced me to look at what love and a loving relationship meant to me. What did I want and what was a deal-breaker? This would mean firmly stepping out of my role as people-pleaser.

I was no longer available to be Amy's emotional support human whenever she felt like she was in the mood to be around me. My new mindset helped establish a clear boundary that we could still potentially have a friendship, if it was equitable, but that was it. I knew it would hurt my heart to end our one-sided romantic relationship. However, I knew it would hurt my soul even more if I continued to stay in it. I would no longer resign myself to being content living in fantasies or daydreams of what could be between us. I was worthy of a beautiful reality.

And Amy was too. Through our twin-flame connection, she found that she could let her guard down with another person and still feel safe. She learned that she could set her own physical boundaries, and that they could be respected rather than negotiated. But perhaps most importantly, once I dropped my people-pleasing and found my voice, she learned why finding a soul connection had possibly evaded her for so long. I called her out on her dating habits. I told her that when she treats everyone she dates like they're just another contestant on some game show to win her love, she would never ever find that one person. Because anyone who accepts that treatment doesn't value themselves enough yet and is not ready for their soulmate. If she wanted real love, she was going to have to slow down and spend time getting to know that person, treating them as if they may be her soul connection, before deciding whether she wanted to pursue a relationship or not. She had to abandon her fear of being alone, while simultaneously reconciling with her fear of commitment. I truly believed that there was someone out there for her and she would find them if she allowed them to see what lay beneath her tough exterior.

The start of that year was a reckoning. I had significant interpersonal work ahead of me. For as much as I had already been through, my coming-out journey was only just beginning.

WHAT'S A LEGO BIN?

It was a very odd time to be us. Chris and I were just coming out of what had been a wonderful holiday season. We had pulled it off, our first major hurdle in this new life: We had spent Thanksgiving and Christmas together knowing that our relationship was over. We had celebrated a wonderful time with the kids and relatives knowing that as a couple we were done. We took some pride in the fact that, with all of our inner turmoil, we had kept our shit together for everyone else's sake.

We were still friends. We could still love each other as friends. We hoped our family members would remember that as we made the decision to come out earlier than anticipated to them. It just made sense to us. While the memories of a beautiful Christmas were still fresh in their heads, we would reveal to them that they had indeed been hanging around with a secret lesbian and her future ex-husband who knew her truth—and everyone had a good time and we all survived it.

It was time to come out. Time for another irrevocable shift.

First came the kids. We all sat down together on the brown fabric couch, me clutching a small piece of paper in one hand that contained my speech and petting the nubby texture of the couch for comfort with the other hand. Hard didn't begin to describe what I was about to do. This would be a moment that could be permanently etched in my children's minds. I didn't want to risk forgetting important words or rambling on an unnecessary tangent, like I was prone to doing.

I took a deep breath, looked at Chris, and then back at the kids. The pressure of tears was already starting to build up. "Kids, Mom and Dad have to tell you something important. Okay? Do you know what a lesbian is?"

Sophie shook her head no while Ollie chimed in with, "What's a Lego bin?"

My inner comedian resisted the urge to say, "Well, son, Mama's got a one-way ticket to Legoland and she ain't never coming back!" Not the time, Jill. Not the time.

"You know how you love a lot of people? Like you love Dad and me, and you love your grandparents and cousins, and maybe you even feel love for your friends," I explained. They nodded their six- and nine-year-old heads. "Well, Mom and Dad still love each other just like you love your family and friends. However, Mom has realized that she is a lesbian. That means that Mom's feelings of romantic love, like what you feel for someone you want to date or marry, are for women and not men." I shifted from talking in the third person and started speaking more like myself. "It has taken me a long time to realize that, while I love your dad, I do not feel the love for him in a way that means we should be married. That means we need to get a divorce, even though we still care for each other and want to be friends."

Sophie began to cry. In her limited knowledge of divorce, the dads always moved far away. We assured her that Dad was not going away and that we would always continue to live in the same town for as long as they were under our care. Once that was clarified, she seemed to take the news better. The mention of Mom being a lesbian merely washed over both of them.

I wondered if including happy lesbian couples in their lives would help them to see that there were many different types of valid loving relationships. I was proud that they would not carry the weight of societal and religious baggage that would come with explaining myself to the older generations. The kids' only request was that we celebrate next year's Christmas together as well. Chris and I agreed, committed to making things work 12 months down the road.

In the scheme of things, coming out to the kids hadn't been that bad. We had made it through. I carried that optimism over to my conversation with my mom. I knew she would most likely struggle with the news, but a small ray of hope within me wondered if possibly she could be happy with me for taking the brave step to live my truth and applaud Chris and me for the mature way in which we were handling our separation. I was wrong. My optimist ducked for cover quickly as our conversation took all sorts of twists and turns, like some nightmarish roller-coaster through the dark where you can't tell which direction you'd be traveling in next. It made me nauseous.

She struggled between trying to keep her cool and sharing that she wasn't really surprised I was gay, and fighting her ever-growing fear that I was destroying the lives of my children and their father. It ping-ponged between being upset that I didn't feel comfortable enough to come out to her first and how I was a deficient parent because of the amount of time I had spent doomscrolling through social media on my cell phone in recent months. What cut the deepest was when she called me *cavalier* about my decision. "I really wish you had thought this through before telling the children," she said. I didn't have the words to express the years and years of thought that had brought me to that moment.

I continued my conversation with her in my mind long after our actual conversation ended, wishing I had told her so much more. I wish she could have known my whole story, particularly what the past several months had been like for me. I wish she could have overheard the conversations Chris and I had and the support I received from him. I wish she could have seen the kids' nonreactive response to me being gay. I wish I could have screamed that life is only hard for gay people because of how others, including family, react with anger, shame, and judgment toward gay people. This didn't have to be so hard. She was making it harder.

I wish she could have known what it felt like for me to have to try and decide between lying to myself and everyone else for the rest of my life for the sake of stability, or accepting my truth and leading us all into the unknown. I wish I had asked her what other choice she thought I had. Where had I erred? Where did I go wrong? I wish I had asked her how she would have handled the situation if she were in my shoes.

What did it matter? She was not in a place to have these discussions. I didn't know if I was either. We were both scared and hurt, but for different reasons. Coming from completely different points of view, it was going to be hard for us to see eye to eye. I wondered if we ever would.

My mom and I didn't speak for a while. When I tried, she would come up with an excuse why she was unable to meet up. She decided she wanted to speak to a therapist for several sessions before she and I talked. When I asked if her "therapist" was a white, male leader at her conservative church, she said yes. I started to abandon hope of building a bridge to her where we could reconnect.

When I didn't receive acceptance from my own mother, I began to abandon any shred of hope I had that things would be okay with Chris's family. But you know what they say about people who assume. I didn't know how I could feel like any more of an ass than I already did for what I was putting everyone through. Chris told his siblings first and the reaction was shocking. They obviously supported him, but they supported me too. For the first time, one of them told me this was "not my fault." They knew it had happened to others. They understood why people hid or were confused by their own sexual orientations. Not being the villain in their eyes was the small reprieve that the heaviness of my heart needed.

And then they did something even more heroic. Knowing that this was most likely not going to go over well with their parents, they told Chris they would be by his side physically as he told his parents, not just in an "I support you and will send you a funny meme if you need" kind of way. They became his protection from people who might inadvertently make hurtful or ignorant remarks. I was still the mother of Chris's children and the woman he had loved for the past two decades. His siblings would be that protective shield to make sure the conversation stayed constructive. And if his parents saw that he was okay with me, and his siblings were okay with me, perhaps they could even be okay with me too.

He never shared the details of their conversation, besides that it involved tears. I imagined them grieving over the end of a marriage that they thought was built to last—their tears an echo of the many tears Chris had shed in the months prior. Nobody wants divorce for their child, and now they were going to go through one that nobody in their circle would have seen coming. Now they had to explain that their future ex-daughter-in-law was a lesbian and nobody ever realized it. I imagined it was a weird thing for them to have to work through.

But the person who seemed to weigh on my heart even more than Chris's siblings and parents was Nana. She had always been my ally, and yet this seemed like the one unforgivable thing I could do that would cut me off from her forever. I didn't want my story told to her through her sister, Chris's mother, or anyone else in the family for that matter. At the same time, I didn't have the guts or the emotional fortitude to risk putting it all out there in a phone call like I did with my mom. I didn't feel it was right for me to drop such heavy news without giving her time to process before responding. I honestly never expected a response.

This was one time in my life when I was immensely grateful for my gift with words. Where my mouth fumbled, my pen scrawled my heart's message across the page with ease. I wrote her a letter sharing what had happened to Chris and me, and the parts people didn't outwardly see. I explained that we had a mutual and deep respect for each other. I told her how knowing I was hurting him was the hardest thing I would ever have to do, but that I was committed to maintaining our friendship and positively co-parenting our children. Most of all, I wanted to let her know that I was still the same person that she had always loved and cared for. I hadn't changed. Everyone just knew a new piece of me now. I told her that I loved her and cared for her and would miss our time together.

Chris gave the note to his mom to hand deliver to her during a trip a few weeks later. Shortly thereafter, I got an unexpected text message. It was from Nana and said, "I love you and you are always welcomed at my home."

Miracles happen. Hearts can change. My hope was renewed that more family bonds would be rebuilt with time. Now that most people in my inner circle knew, I could turn some of my attention back to figuring out how to end the one life I had known and start another life from scratch.

STAGE SIX

FINDING NEW STRENGTH

THE COST OF TACOS

"Middle-aged, minivan-driving, homeschooling lesbian mom seeks fellow middle-aged lesbian who likes kids (but maybe doesn't have their own), and enjoys the finer points of wearing sweatpants, eating take-out Thai food, and watching mushroom documentaries or reality cooking competitions on TV. Must tolerate dad jokes and the occasional snort while sleeping. Cute butts are a plus."

I was curious what would happen if I made that my dating profile. Would there be a person out there who, while clad in their gray Under Armour sweats, would see that on their phone and think, *I've met my match!*? I doubted it. Quite frankly, I didn't know who would want me or who was even out there. Amy didn't want me, and I was finally in a place of accepting that. The truth of the matter was, I didn't really want her either. Even still, the thought of putting myself out there in the big queer dating pool was terrifying. This was it. Training wheels off. It was time to lesbian with the real lesbians.

One of Chris's buddies who was well-versed in the world of adult online dating gave him a valuable tip. He said to *always* go for the paid version of the app. Knowing that our assets and bank account would soon be divided in half, the thought of shelling out a dime for a site that could be used for free seemed idiotic at first. I questioned the value of the $15 per month membership. Although it would allow me access to more profiles and better filters to find matches more suited for me, and give me some flexibility when I accidentally swiped away someone I meant to show interest in, I didn't know if it was really necessary. I would just have to find my person among the free options.

Then, I pulled up my bank account and noticed that I had recently spent more than that amount to buy tacos for lunch. His advice clicked.

Here I was, searching for a life partner on this app, and questioning if it was worth as much as one taco lunch. Oof. I shelled out the money for the subscription and made myself lunch at home that day.

I wrote myself a profile. And then deleted it. And rewrote it. And deleted it. It felt like the weirdest marketing assignment I had ever been given: sell myself to potential dating prospects without coming across as desperate or egotistical, or both. In the end, I kept it basic, with the core things people should know about me. Things that mattered to me, but also just the right lack of information to spark some intrigue. I started with a nice headshot and natural smile, one where the wrinkles around my eyes would be visible enough to indicate that the under-30 crowd need not apply. The picture was at a beach with palm trees in the background. Look at me, being so cool and nature-like. I'm going to snag me a nature lesbian!

Next was a picture of me sitting on my brother's porch swing with a beer and his dog in the background. Lesbians love beer and dogs. This will get me some swipes, I thought. I hoped the fact that I didn't actually enjoy beer and didn't actually own that dog, or any dog, wouldn't be a deterrent once I reached the conversation portion of the dating experience. I rationalized that the photo was to demonstrate my tolerance of both.

My last picture, though, caused a real internal debate. It was a shot of the kids and me standing at the top of a summit during our most recent camping adventure in the Great Smoky Mountains. Our backs were turned to the camera, but the photo made it clear that I was a mom with two young kids. I wondered if I should include the photo in my profile. Perhaps that was a detail, like the beer and dog truth, that I could just drop on someone later after they were head over heels in love with me.

Is that the person I would want to date, I thought? *No,* I told myself. I have to include this picture. It would be my own personal way of filtering for a partner who would be okay with what mattered most to me, my kids. Anyone who would not swipe right on me because of that picture was not my person. I knew I was setting myself up for far fewer matches.

With my new profile in place, I decided to go on my own swipe hunt and quickly realized why Amy and others had complained about the wild world of lesbian online dating. It was fraught with problematic profiles. The first thing that threw me was the number of women posting pictures of themselves with filters. "Janet, you are *not* a rat covered in stardust!" I screamed at my phone, completely confused as to why a grown adult seeking a dating partner would toss on a filter that gave them a pink nose, whiskers, and glittery orbs abounding. I wondered what regular old Janet looked like and why she wasn't okay with just showing herself in her normal human state. She wouldn't be arriving to a date dressed like a magical rodent, would she?

Aside from the incredible number of filtered photos that danced across my phone, I was also shocked by the duck-lip photos and the tongue-licking-things photos. Perhaps I was a bad lesbian, but the unnatural nature of the pictures was not attractive to me. I would have preferred someone make a goofy face so that I could see their sense of humor, instead of their attempt at a seductive men's magazine pose. My friends reminded me that not everyone on the app was looking for a life partner. Some just want sex. Depending on the day, I questioned what category I was looking for too.

The trifecta of frustration, when I would find an unfiltered and non-ducked headshot, was that typically by the time I got to a person's last photo it was one of them and their husband. They were seeking a third to add to their relationship. The dating pool was smaller than I could have imagined. With each profile that I passed on, my desperation grew. I was never going to find my person, and I was never going to get my taco lunch because I had just blown the money on this app. I did what people do in dating and started to lower my standards. I swiped right on more people and started conversations with some, trying to contort their words in my mind to be something that I would like to hear. Instead of looking for red flags, I looked for glimmers of hope: things I could love about them to ignore the fact that their partying lifestyle or smoking habits were incompatible with my life. If they looked successful and self-confident, I tried to overlook the negativity or rudeness in their messages. They usually sensed the mismatch first and ghosted me.

I did go on a few nice dates. I was encouraged that there were interesting and attractive women out there. However, I also realized that, just like in heterosexual dating, being a lesbian doesn't mean you have chemistry with every woman—even if they are interesting and attractive. I tried to make some things work that just didn't. When I got stood up just 30 minutes before a date because it was raining outside and she didn't want to go out, I realized that I was upset because I had blocked out my calendar and spent precious hours of kid-free time to get dressed up for this person. When she asked me to reschedule, I was so very close to saying yes, but I realized if I did that, I was not loving myself properly. Loneliness and fear were making me compromise what mattered to me. I was stretching myself for a woman who wouldn't even walk through rain for me. I was worth more than that.

And now I felt disgusted in myself again. What had I just done? I had blown up my life for the chance to date women and find someone I could love with my whole heart. And here I was taking whatever came my way. It wasn't their fault. I didn't know what I wanted to begin with, so I just said yes to most people. And holy crap! This was a pattern that had repeated my whole life, including my early career and my wedding. When I wasn't honest and clear about what I wanted in life, I let other people steer my path for me. I was ready to stop that now. It was time to be the captain of my own ship and take ownership of the direction I was heading. This captain was going to need a map, and this map came in the shape of a small, black, pleather-bound notebook with a sticker Agnieszka had given me with some sacred geometry circles that said "Expect a Miracle."

I stared at those overlapping circles, the symbolism of unity and connectedness in the universe, and brushed the cover with my fingertips, realizing my own state of internal disconnect. Up until this point, my dating experience had been ego-driven. Coming out left me feeling wounded. I was desperate to feel loved or admired by someone. My search thus far had been for some queen or Joan of Arc type to save me. I had fallen for the idea of being swept off my feet. What I really needed was to stand firmly in my own, with a partner by my side doing the same.

It was time to rediscover Jill. I took time to meditate daily. I reconnected with the divine energy that had been there to support me in the most magnificent of ways throughout my life. My faith and optimism began to fill me again as I realized that I would find my partner once I knew who I was and who I wanted my partner to be. Because a partnership is just that: two people who add value to each other. I began the journey to recognize my value.

I felt overcome by a strong compulsion one morning to create my ideal partner. I opened that black notebook and began to write. The words flowed to my mind faster than they could come out of my black ink pen. I scrawled as quickly as I could, feeling only brief moments of guilt for designing a person on paper who I wanted in my life. I wondered if I was being vain. My brain would pepper me with thoughts that I was dreaming too big or asking too much as I wrote all of the qualities that my ideal person would possess. Now I laugh at the thought that my brain tried to put limitations on what I was allowed to dream or envision. Dreaming is not the time to think small. My heart knew better, and I continued to write as fast as the thoughts came to me. My heart knew who I wanted, even if the rest of me didn't know if she actually existed.

I wrote pages and pages of description that day. Everything from "a massive smile that could light up a room" to "the ability to love my children as her own." I wanted her to live a healthy lifestyle and for our knowledge and skills in health to complement each other. I wanted someone to take walks with. I wanted to be close in age. She'd be a good snuggler. Someone who liked peaceful home decor and fuzzy blankets. Playful sex and passionate kissing. Thai food and sweatpants. She would be athletic, but not overly intense. A nonsmoker who enjoyed a casual drink every so often. Both intelligent and goofy. Someone with the ability to continually grow and improve as a person. She wouldn't be religious but would be spiritual. She would read books and go on adventures, but not suggest biking or concerts. Most importantly, she would be kind. I must have written the word *kind* at least six times as I described my ideal partner. I wanted my heart to meet another heart and feel right at home.

I didn't know if this person existed, but now I didn't care. I knew what I wanted and that became the new bar by which I evaluated my dating prospects. Now I was dating with my heart instead of my head. I was ready to expect a miracle.

Very quickly my frustration returned. My person was not here, but at least now I was no longer going to force connections that I knew were doomed from the start. I contemplated giving up dating altogether and becoming a nun. If I could be whole and complete in myself, I wouldn't need another person. I decided at the very least that I would delete the dating app for now. With everything I had on my plate at the moment—coming out to more friends and family, figuring out my divorce, and running a business with my future ex-husband—I didn't need to add the stress of starting a new relationship. I opened the dating app on my phone to cancel my subscription.

And then I saw her.

U-HAULING

Delete, Jill.

Shut up, brain.

Delete, Jill.

Okay, just one more picture.

De-fucking-lete the app, Jillian.

But what if . . . yes . . . look at this!

That smile. The massive one that could light up a room was there stretched across my phone screen. It was just so pretty and toothy and perfect. Her eyes were arched into tiny crescent moons, like happiness was bursting from each cell of her body. It was so genuine and real. I couldn't help but smile back.

And the next picture? Her in a Buffalo Bills knit cap. *Holy crap, Universe! She's from Western New York too?* What were the odds that we would both be from the same place and now living in a new same place? Her last picture was a headshot of her lying on a beach towel with aviator glasses on, the sun glistening on her tanned skin and sporty blond hair. I looked around the room for hidden cameras. This felt like a setup. Where had she been this whole time? Why was she just appearing now as I was about to make my grand departure from the lesbian world of dating? How had the app read my notebook?

Her name was just listed as J. She was three years older than me and only 17 miles away, according to the app. She liked dogs. Didn't smoke. Social drinker. No comment positive or negative about kids. I noticed she had adopted my strategy: give them just enough information to filter, but leave some mystery. Well played, J.

My head made one final attempt to delete the app before my heart swiped right on J. *One last time,* I told myself. And then, like some strange magic, I got a notification that she accepted my swipe. She liked me back. It had never happened that fast. We were now connected and on to the next stage. Time for one of us to make an attempt at brilliance. I started.

"You're a Bills fan, which is a pretty reliable indicator that you're a good person." (Attentive compliment box checked.)

"So what part of WNY are you from?" (Things we have in common box checked.)

"Oops. I probably should have started with a 'Hi! How are you?'" (Awkward box checked.)

I waited. She typed.

"Nope . . . talking about the Bills is actually the perfect way to open up a conversation. :)"

We were off to a good start. I had a good feeling about this. The left ventricle of my heart high-fived the right ventricle of my heart for a job well done.

J and I chatted back and forth with ease. She was a chiropractor and nutritionist. She wasn't from Buffalo but had studied there. She wasn't a beer fan, but loved kombucha. She didn't have kids, but had always wanted them. My eyes couldn't believe what I was reading. Did I just manifest my dream woman? Yes. Did I leave off one vitally important piece in my manifesting exercise? Also, yes. Geography.

The app wasn't wrong. J was only 17 miles away from me that day, but only because she was in town for a nutrition conference. Home was in Pennsylvania, a scant 936.3 miles away. My brain laughed at my heart, and I told J we could stop talking. I was clearly a dating dead-end.

Now any experienced lesbians reading this book right now are probably smirking. There are a few things about lesbian dating culture that I learned quickly: (1) women fall fast and hard for each other, developing emotional bonds quickly, (2) first dates can last for days or years, (3) U-Hauling is a very real phenomenon, with couples cohabitating in record times practically unheard of in the hetero world, and (4) geography is never a limitation when it comes to women loving women.

I was aware of these stereotypes and overly cautious not to fall into any of them. I had heard the horror stories of unhealthy attachments and bad behaviors that could result from settling down at a record pace. I warned myself that no matter how good someone felt, that the early high from dating would eventually wear off. I had to make sure I was in love with the person and not in love with the idea of being with the person. And if my person lived 936.3 miles away, and I was tied to Florida because I had promised my children I would never move away from their dad, then what was the point of pursuing anything?

"I like how real you are," J continued. "Sometimes it's hard to find people who can carry on a conversation on here. So . . . if you're cool with it, I'd like to keep chatting." I agreed. I had to admit that I enjoyed chatting with her too. If anything, it was easier now that the pressure was off. We could talk like friends instead of potential partners. I found that conversing came more easily without that expectation in mind. We wished each other a good night and picked up where we left off in the morning.

J eventually told me her name was Jen. She laughed because her best friend growing up was named Jill. I laughed because my best friend growing up was named Jen. We were both Aries and obsessed with the show *Boy Meets World* in our youth. Jen B shared a birthday with my dear deceased grandmother, Jean B. We knew a mutual person in common in Buffalo. I really, really liked her. It was too bad this would never work out.

On her last day in Florida, Jen invited me over to hang out by the pool of the Airbnb that she was renting with friends. She had nothing to do, and it just so happened that Chris would be with the kids that day. After the amount of stress I had been under, perhaps a lazy day at the pool with this adorable new friend of mine would be just what I needed. I wanted to smile at her humongous smile.

When I arrived, she had prepared a plate of cut vegetables with beet hummus as a snack for us. What an odd food choice to lead with. But also, I loved beets and hummus. How did she know? She poured me a kombucha with vodka and lime. I loved those too. How did she know? I looked around once again for spy cameras, wondering how my manifesting notebook could have created someone who also loved beets and booch. I wondered if I would ever find someone like her who lived closer.

Our conversations took a deep dive quickly as she asked very specific questions about my life.

"So you were married to a man?"

"Yes."

"And are you still?"

"Technically, yes."

"Are you planning on getting a divorce?"

"Absolutely."

"Have you filed the paperwork?"

"Er, not yet," I fibbed. The truth was we hadn't even started the paperwork.

She looked concerned. I wondered if she had been in this situation before and gotten burned. My red flag was waving in the breeze at her.

"And you both still live together in the same house?"

"Yes . . . I . . . we're in separate bedrooms," I stumbled to include, as if that didn't make the situation any more uncomfortable for her. For the first time, I started to feel bad that I had even put myself on a dating app at this point. Jen deserved better than what I was offering to her right now. My current marital and housing situation suddenly felt like I was being incredibly disrespectful toward her. I knew I would have to get some ducks in a row before I pursued any real dating with anyone.

She nodded politely and took another sip of her drink. "These situations can be complicated," she said. I exhaled at her empathy. She made me want to do better. Our conversation moved away from my messy status and covered every other area possible. We talked about work, our health beliefs, energy, Boo Berry cereal, our families, the coming-out experience, places on our travel bucket lists, books, old TV shows, favorite spots around Buffalo, our introverted and awkward nature, and our perfect height difference of two inches. We ordered Thai food for dinner and her friends, back from a long day of golf, joined us and shared hilarious tales of their previous adventures together with Jen. Jen inched her chair toward me and took my hand under the table as they talked. It fit perfectly in mine, like two puzzle pieces notched together. Her friends asked how long we had known each other, surprised that the answer was just hours rather than days or years. "You just seem really comfortable together," they said. It was true and I felt validated that they noticed it too.

After her friends had politely retired to bed, she and I ended the date with a solid session of making out on the couch like teenagers. I liked the natural spearmint lip balm that she reapplied every so often. She gave me the mostly used tube as a parting gift. I hoped that the scent could bring me back to that moment with her. I wanted anything that would keep the memory of this day alive. And then, like Cinderella at the ball, it was over. Time for me to don my kerchief and return to cleaning a house and caring for humans, without the help of friendly woodland creatures or fairy god people. She had a flight to catch.

We stood by the front door and hugged every cell of our being into each other. The hug turned from feelings of affection and contentment to feelings of sadness and desperation at the realization that our one and only date was over. She squeezed me tighter and all I could whisper in her ear was a faint, "We'll figure it out." We felt the same. This was something different, like neither of us had experienced before. I knew I wanted to be in her energy and she in mine. I knew we had millions of more conversations ahead of us that might never happen once geographical distance set in.

I exited the door and walked down the stairs to my van, and she waved one last good-bye and disappeared out of sight. Ugh. It was really over. I sat there in the darkness of my van for a moment, not ready to give up how I felt about this day with her. I tried to reengage my mind back into the reality of my life and what was on my to-do list for tomorrow with the kids and the bar. As I plugged my phone into the charger a message popped up.

"You forgot your water bottle," Jen texted. YES! We weren't done. I had lost my glass slipper and she found it in the nick of time.

"I'm still here," I replied. "I'll come back in and grab it."

As I approached the stairs, I noticed she had already changed into her pajamas. Her sleepy smile greeted me in her baggy gray sweatpants and a marled blue Buffalo Bills T-shirt, her blond hair messily flopping on her head with each step down. My heart skipped and I walked up the steps to meet her one last time. I took the water bottle from her hand, intentionally brushing my fingers against hers to soak in a little more touch. We joined in one last hug and kiss, she one step above me so that she had to bend lower to reach me this time. "Thank you, Jen," I said as I watched her slowly return back upstairs. I turned around and got quietly back into my car. That was it. Our time together was now officially done.

As I drove home my eyes looked up at the vast starry sky and I felt compelled to give thanks for this wonderful soul that had been brought into my life. I had manifested my dream human. How lucky was I! Even if it was just a day, I was so grateful to have had that day with her. It was one I would remember.

I wondered how long we would continue texting. I didn't know how we could possibly have a future with our lives so deeply rooted in our current hometowns, but I didn't want to think about not continuing where we left off. I told her we would figure it out, but I had no idea what that meant or how we would do it. I decided to keep faith in the unknown and trust that it would work out.

I wish I could say that it was easy to maintain that faith. The truth is that within 20 minutes, those tears of happiness quickly turned to hot, burning tears of anger. What if she wasn't brought into my life like a cosmic reward for being brave and living my truth? What if this was some sort of cruel joke? I imagined some mastermind in the clouds laughing as I had been gifted the human I wanted most, only to lose them. It now felt like punishment. "You want to see what it's like to have love ripped away?!" I imagined them saying. After what I had done to Chris, taking love from him, now I would have to live with that same hurt. *This is what I deserved,* I told myself.

That sentiment didn't feel right, though, either. I didn't want to believe that this higher power was a scorekeeper, penalizing me for behaviors that members of our earthly society deemed sinful or vile. These new thoughts of reward and punishment were not coming from a higher power; they were coming from the dark place of fear within me. I was punishing myself. I was assuming that I wouldn't be allowed to be happy in the future because of the guilt I carried about my separation from Chris. Deep breath. I had to remember the good that could come of this for both of us. We would both be allowed to find love again, someone we could each love with our whole hearts and feel that love reciprocated.

I made a note to myself to specify a zip code in my next manifesting exercise.

MODERN FAMILY

Find purpose in this.

This is a phrase I tell myself when difficult things happen and I don't have an explanation as to why. Seek the lesson to be learned. Look for the facet of my personality that I have been able to exercise and make stronger from this experience. Discover the new perspective gained from what happened. For me, finding purpose has always helped make hard things more tolerable.

I had to know why Jen came into my life and why she had to return to 936.3 miles out of my life. There had to be a reason that the Universe brought me the person I had dreamed of on paper and also set us up for a long-distance relationship, a lesbian dating stereotype that I had vowed to avoid so as not to give fuel to the belief. But here I was, looking up which credit cards had the best airline miles programs. Was there really a purpose to my person being located so far away?

It didn't take long for the purpose of this situation to become clear: I wanted Jen, but I had to know that I didn't need Jen. I was no longer looking for someone to complete me. I wanted someone to complement me. I had to be whole. I had to learn how to stand on my own two feet. I still had so much to process and so many things to work through.

While Jen didn't need me to be "done" processing (because, let's be honest, when is that work ever really done), she did need to see that I was doing the work to get there. And work assignment number one was to make myself free and clear for the dating. It was time to face the piece I had been pushing to the back burner. Chris and I needed to start the divorce process.

It's hard to have a good vibration around the word *divorce*. There would be no way to carve apart two lives and have it be easy, even if Chris and I were on good terms and willing to communicate. But we weren't ready to let our lives devolve into the dirty horror story that divorce can create. The eternal optimist in me asked, *What if we could create our own definition of divorce?*

What would a good divorce look like? I wondered if I could envision an ideal divorce in the same way I had envisioned my ideal partner. I didn't know if it was possible, but I figured there could be no harm in trying. I would have to break open the constraints on what I knew divorces to be like and imagine what they could be instead.

To have a good divorce, Chris and I would need a mutual goal. Divorce wouldn't have to be a total lose-lose situation if we had a goal that we could both work toward and achieve in the process. For us, there could be no greater goal than creating a stable, loving environment for our children between two homes. Keeping their needs at the forefront of our decision-making would allow both of us to make difficult concessions that we might otherwise be unwilling to make.

A secondary goal was for us to maintain our friendship. We wondered if, down the road, we would be able to attend events and holidays together, each of us with our new partners, like one big modern family. It seemed like a stretch, but we were tired of putting limitations on what we could and couldn't do, what we were allowed to have and not allowed to have. As I shed the expectations of my living a normal hetero life, I was also ready to shed the expectation that divorce had to be a complete disaster.

We chose to insulate ourselves from outsider opinions as much as possible when going through the divorce process, not wanting to be tainted by others' perceptions. Instead, we proceeded with the mindset and mantra that "we control our definition of divorce." Rather than go the traditional lawyer approach, we both worked with a mutual lawyer friend of ours who was aligned with our goal of an amicable split. He mediated our separation and helped us reason with each other, rather than drag out a winless fight over who deserved what. He reminded us that in divorce both people will lose things. Even if they feel like they're winning, they still give up something. He encouraged us to protect our energetic and emotional capital, recognizing that those had immense value too.

I know mediation is not always an option in divorce. Chris and I had the benefit in our divorce of mutual respect and friendship. We had 20 years of history that we weren't ready to quickly erase over fighting about nitty-gritty details like who would pay for the Netflix account and who would take our beloved $12 stove-top espresso percolator. In all divorce situations, good or bad, there are always a few things that are within our control. The most important of these things is our mindset.

Now, I don't want to mislead anyone into believing that if you throw enough fairy dust on a divorce that it will magically become some masterpiece of societal uncoupling. Even in the best-case scenario, there is a lot to process. But I had faith, deep down, that after all was said and done, his life and my life could return to a state of beauty, and perhaps be even more beautiful and love-filled than what we had previously known. We could both move forward in different directions and create futures with fulfillment. I had an undying optimism that maybe one day my children would be surrounded by four loving and supportive parents instead of two. When they say, "It takes a village," we would make our own family village.

Some expressed concern for this village, upset that our children would potentially be raised in a two-woman household. (Gasp! What an unstable home with all that estrogen floating around!) I struggled with the logic of understanding how that could be less optimal than me raising my children as a single parent. If one mom was good, wouldn't two moms be even better?

I resisted the urge to share the many research studies that found that children raised in same-sex households fared at least the same when it came to academic performance and emotional well-being as opposite-sex households. But I knew it wouldn't matter if I shared the American Psychological Association's conclusion that "there is no scientific evidence that parenting effectiveness is related to parental sexual orientation: lesbian and gay parents are as likely as heterosexual parents to provide supportive and healthy environments for their children."[5] The feelings of those who feared same-sex households were not based on research or logic. It was their visceral response of fear and the belief that I was living my life in a substandard way.

There were days when the reality of my life at this point left me wanting to crawl into bed to hide. Most days I felt scared about how I would make ends meet and provide for my kids. Some days I grieved the ease of our former life together. There were days when the emotions felt so big, I didn't know if or when I'd surface from being pulled so deep under the waves of despair. In those moments when I felt like I was drowning, I resorted to my fallback of finding the purpose. I wanted to believe that, unknown future aside, even within our divorce process there could be benefits gained. The important lesson for me was that divorce does not have to be a division whose parts are less than and inferior to the previous whole.

The first and most notable improvement in our lives was the drastic increase in our quality time with each other. When I came out to Chris that day in our bar, he was deeply wounded and knew he needed time to recover. At the corporate job where he worked in addition to the bar, his boss was a single mom who was empathetic to the weight of what he was going through. She suggested he take time off and then work remotely once he felt ready. His old schedule had been heading to the office before the kids woke up, followed by evenings working at our bar until long after they were both asleep. I remember a nearly 10-day stretch in the month prior to coming out to him when he rarely saw us for more than a few minutes at a time.

Now, armed with the knowledge that a divorce was inevitably in our future, he began to be more intentional about spending time with the kids. They played board games and basketball, watched movies and built Lego creations. For the first time, he joined us on one of our homeschool group's camping trips to the Florida Keys. It was an awkward trip, given that only two other people on the trip knew of our situation and the fact that we slept in separate beds within the tent, but we had quality moments together. We were making up for lost time.

Months later, when we reached the point of living in separate households, I began to find other new benefits. The fear of having to do everything on my own turned to empowerment. The dread of thinking *This is* all *on me* turned to the excitement of realizing that *This* is *all on me*. This was the time to educate myself. Take control. Steer my own course. Did I want to learn more about personal finances and investing and save more toward retirement? *Yes*! Did I want to fill my house with minimal furniture and maximum houseplants? *Yes*! I taught myself to mow the grass, take care of the pool, find a good high-yield savings account, buy stocks, apply solar film to my house's windows, check the oil level in my car—things that I had relegated to "not my skill set" in the past. Here I was, reclaiming them and doing them as best I could.

Having time away from the kids also made me a better mother. The toll from years of trying to run a business while being glued to my homeschooled children 24/7, left me burned out and disconnected. We were rich in time together, but poor in quality time. Knowing that I would have a few days of respite every other week to get caught up on work, have grown-up time with friends, and sleep as long as my body needed, gave my children a recharged version of their mom. Their homeschool studies became more interesting as I found renewed creativity and the energy for us to explore together. I astonished myself at the amount of work I could get done in my kid-free hours, so that when we were back together we had time for play and to ride roller-coasters at our local amusement park until we felt sick.

My children were no longer getting the version of me that limped along from day to day, praying for a break. Their happy mom was starting to come back. I committed to being intentional with our time together from here on out. There was purpose to this all.

A GOOD WAY TO DIE

Since I was a kid, I've had a powerful thought that would arise in my brain every so often. It was interesting when it would pop up because it didn't appear like a conscious thought that was generated by my own mind. It always felt like an outsider was talking, but from within me. It felt like the thought was a piece of paper that someone added to my brain with a note that said, "You are going to die before you turn 40. Kind regards, Your Soul."

Over the years, I had different reactions to this thought.

Sometimes it was disbelief. I would tell myself that I couldn't die that young—I had things to do on this Earth, like become a business mogul, learn how to steam artichokes, and track down the members of New Kids on the Block to finally get an autograph.

Sometimes I felt relief at the thought of an early and untimely death, especially during my teenage years. My perfectionist self worked so hard and felt so stressed at times that death by 40 sounded like the literal light at the end of the tunnel.

Sometimes I felt ambivalent about the idea. Die by 40? Sure. I'll clear my agenda and blow my retirement funds on organic coffee and fuzzy socks.

When I became a parent, the feelings turned to sadness. Death by 40? But my kids are so young! Their hearts will hurt. That will put too much on Chris. I can't die. I have a responsibility to them.

As I meandered through my 30s, the gut feeling of my untimely demise loomed heavier each year. I knew it was coming. I felt it in my bones. It was an unchangeable truth. I believed it so much that by 35 I started to get my affairs in order for the inevitable. I had just been handed something that was already meant to happen. In some ways I thought I was lucky. At least I had the heads-up that my time here on Earth would be limited. I felt bad for those people who thought they would live a long life, only to have it unexpectedly cut short. They never saw it coming. I wondered if maybe they would live differently knowing that their future was only a few more days or a few more years, instead of a few more decades. I wondered why I denied myself pleasures and experiences in this lifetime as well. I chalked it up to still needing to be sensible and rational and not letting on to others that my hourglass would be running out. Even with death approaching, there were so many years that I wouldn't allow myself to fully live.

I secretly organized paperwork and made a list of passwords that Chris might need after my passing. I wrote a note to my children to let them know how much I loved them and how amazing their lives would be and how fulfilling and rich in experience my own life had been.

I sobbed while writing it. Death was coming and I didn't know how it would happen or how long I had left. Sometimes, when I would step on a plane, drive on a crowded highway, or eat raw seafood, I would occasionally be visited by the thought, *Is this it? Is this how I go?* In hindsight, this all sounds a bit extreme to me. But at the time, this felt like as much of my truth as anything else I knew about myself.

After coming out to my mom, our conversations remained sporadic. Our daily phone calls and weekly visits had become a memory. The arrival of COVID-19 in the midst of all of this and subsequent quarantining of the world at least meant that I didn't have to tie our distance entirely on my coming out. I could convince myself that even if we wanted to be closer, we just weren't allowed to at that time. It was for our own safety. I wondered if COVID-19 would be the thing that took me out.

The forced distance between me and the rest of the world was in some ways an inadvertent blessing. It allowed me time to process my recent coming out, explore my new identity, and handle divorce proceedings without the obligations of social, family, or work events where I might have to reveal myself as a lesbian to more people. Even in my newness to it, I was already tired of "coming out" and appreciated the reprieve.

As days of distance turned into weeks, my mom decided to reach out with a lengthy e-mail, a way to begin the process of reconnecting. I was hoping for those words of loving support that I longed to hear. Maybe even a "How are you holding up, Tiger?" I hoped she might have started to realize the mounting stress I might be under from coming out, ending a marriage, beginning a long-distance relationship, homeschooling two children through a pandemic, and keeping our bar financially afloat when we were no longer allowed to open our doors. I laughed, wondering what kind of cherry the Universe could top this crappy sundae with. Maybe a rare off-season hurricane? Perhaps alligators would learn how to use laser beam guns? It didn't have to be so big. My coffee maker breaking could have been the straw that broke the camel's back at that point. I was fragile.

Her conversation never went there. Instead, she focused on how our relationship had decayed and how I seemed to be doing little to revive it. She was hurting because of my life choices, and I was not fixing it. The truth was, I didn't know how to fix it. I didn't even know if fixing it was my job. It's hard to know how to fix something when you don't understand the root of why it broke in the first place. How had my truth caused her pain? My heart craved care, and instead I was being asked to give care. I wondered if my brave front of "I am happy" and "things are going to be okay" was perhaps a bit too convincing. Perhaps I was holding it together too well. She couldn't see that I was hollow and had nothing left to give.

My blurry eyes read and reread the final part of her e-mail. "What happened to us?" it asked. "I remember you saying a while back that you had this premonition that you were going to die before you were 40. For me, it feels like you have."

I was dumbstruck. Though I was managing to hold things together in that period of time, I was changing as a person. It was impossible not to change. Life was testing me in so many new ways, and it was my time to figure out what I was really made of. The old Jill would have crumbled from the stress. She would have beaten herself up over the lack of people-pleasing that coming out as gay causes.

The people were not pleased. The old Jill would have sacrificed herself for the care of others until she was physically ill. She would have overworked herself to feel like she was enough. The old Jill would have poured her energy into making her life look like everything was hunky-dory so that people wouldn't worry about her or her family. The old Jill would have done whatever she had to do to avoid making waves.

Mom was right. The old Jill would never have survived this. That Jill was gone.

And so, that was my death. It had happened, but not in the terrible, scary, or potentially gory ways I had imagined over the years. My fear around death lifted as I realized that my vision had in fact come true. That voice in my head was now satisfied. The thoughts of an early death were gone, never to return. I had just turned 39 years old five days prior.

I responded to her. "Maybe it is a death of the old Jill, though that seems a little dramatic. I prefer to see it as a healed Jill."

I was ready for a new beginning.

SAVING SANDCASTLES AND HUNTING BLUEBIRDS

Have you ever had a conversation with someone and wondered, *Could this be God?* The way they speak to you. The way they look at you. The way you feel around them. Whenever this thought enters my mind, I notice that it's always about someone I wouldn't expect.

It's the person you almost passed by at the coffee shop and then end up having a conversation with. It's the child at the playground who approached you to push them on the swings. It's the person seeking shelter at the airport arrival area, hoping someone will give them some money to catch the bus or grab a bite to eat. While it's my belief that God or Spirit or the Universe lives in everyone, there are times when the God in someone else seems to also see the God in me, and they have a conversation. To me, it's a constant reminder that the Universe is always looking out for me, so long as I am keeping myself open to receiving.

I was at the stage in my coming out known as the "messy middle." The name always struck me as a bit humorous since the "middle" seems to start immediately after the initial elation of taking the brave leap to come out to oneself—and accepting and loving oneself for it—and lasts until you begin to feel like you're on stable ground again. The messy middle is wet sand on a beach. It pulls you down, making your journey require extra effort with each step. It's unstable. But it's doable if you pace yourself and stay hydrated.

My messy middle started when I had that first conversation with Tisa and the glass of Jack Daniel's. It was now over a year later and I was tired of walking. The journey had gotten harder. Chris had moved out. The future of our small business and my income was uncertain. We had nearly completed our divorce paperwork but had yet to file it, tired of trying to figure out details like where the kids would attend school in the coming year—between our two households or whether I could continue to homeschool.

The reality that many of my family members were no longer speaking to me began to hit harder. The space between Chris and me grew. My bank account dwindled. While I was grateful for my relationship with Jen, like a ray of sunshine through a cloudy beach day, the physical distance between us made those everyday steps feel lonely and arduous.

I began to go into a bit of a tailspin as I observed the life I knew crumble around me. It was like watching a sandcastle on the beach quickly erode with the rising tide, entire walls of the structure crashing down into the waves. I was aware that the castle of my life couldn't survive any longer as I knew it. It still didn't prevent me from trying to hold tight to the sand as it slipped through my fingers. Everything I had built would be gone soon and I was terrified. Coming out as LGBTQ+ is hard enough in and of itself. Coming out as an adult has the unique challenge of an almost certain upheaval of life. I wished I knew everything would be okay, but I didn't. I was full of fear, worry, and occasional moments of regret for leaving a life that was relatively easy. I could feel myself falling back into that dissociated state, wanting to hide under my weighted blanket and not do life anymore.

Sometimes the Universe works through people, but sometimes the Universe needs the help of Facebook to put the messages back in front of your face. My message came to me in the form of a post from my favorite spiritual mystic, Kerin Monaco, who popped back into my life many months after my reading about Amy. She had started a membership called the Wild-Hearted Collective, an eclectic group of women from around the world seeking a way to better connect with their spiritual guides. The women were into tarot cards, astrology, planet retrogrades, spiritual archetypes, and all sorts of other things that I had almost no knowledge of. For most of my life, I would have felt out of place in this group, like an impostor. But in that moment, I didn't. My life was crumbling; my ego was gone. What was left of me just wanted help and, for some reason, this group seemed like exactly who I wanted to be surrounded by.

What I loved about the group was that Kerin was not our guru on the stage, the spiritual head who would channel and interpret messages for us mere mortals. Kerin recognized that we were all connected to the energy of the Universe and sometimes just needed help and support to trust that connection. The message I received over and over again was that my spiritual guides were there to support me and surround me. If I had the courage to leap and the bravery to trust, I would be caught.

Kerin encouraged us to hone our own channeling skills through meditation and journaling. She encouraged us to play and challenge our faith in our guides. "Pick something really specific that you want your spiritual guides to show you and see how that appears to you." When I accepted that challenge, I decided I wanted to see a bluebird, like the beautiful one that perched itself on Jen's windowsill during my latest trip to her home. This was a bird that I had not seen in Florida before. Blue jays, yes. Fluffy round chubby bluebirds, no. I smirked at the impossible task I had asked of my guides.

The day pressed on and there were no bluebirds. My smirk faded and began to change to desperation at asking them for such a ridiculous request. Maybe I wasn't opening my mind enough or allowing more artistic leeway. Maybe my "bluebird" would instead appear as a blue painted bird, like a heron or egret, on a neighborhood sign or billboard. I began looking desperately for that blue bird. Any bluish bird. I tried to convince myself that a gray one may look blue in a certain light. I pushed. I started taking a scenic route on my drive home to give myself better odds. Clearly my spirit guides weren't going to show me, so I went searching for it. And guess what? I never found it.

At home that night, I felt like I failed. What worked for Kerin and some of the other Wild-Hearted women didn't work for me. Maybe I wasn't believing hard enough or correct enough. Maybe my spirit guides weren't looking out for me. Maybe I didn't even deserve to ask for something so frivolous and foolish. They had cancers to heal and burning towns to save. My creator didn't have time for me.

I walked to the kitchen to prepare me and Sophie mugs of chamomile tea before bed. Honey dripped on the countertop, and I realized that we were out of paper towels in the kitchen to clean it up. I flicked on the light in the garage to grab a new roll and, in my exhaustion, knocked the package of several rolls onto the floor. Ugh. Another obstacle to keep me from my favorite part of life during this period—the time when I was asleep. As I bent to pick up the fallen paper towels and put them back on the shelf, my eyes caught an opaque plastic bin full of miscellaneous household items that I had packed up years ago in an attempt to declutter: a vintage Japanese tea set that my brother gifted to me one Christmas, a few tin beer signs given to Chris after we opened our bar, and my grandmother's old cookie jar, which looked like a tree stump. I pulled the bin out farther to see what other treasures from my past were buried inside and found myself face to face with the lid of that tree stump cookie jar. On it was a ceramic bluebird. I stared at its chubby, cheerful little face in disbelief and my eyes filled with tears. How could I have forgotten about that bird? I had seen it a million times in my childhood. And there it was, back in front of me again covered in a thin layer of garage dust.

That was the lesson I needed. I was not alone. And when I stopped pushing and trying to control the outcome, things could happen for me. I wondered what was waiting for me if I let the waves roll in and didn't try to hold the sandcastle together. What if my world wasn't crumbling around me? What if I was being gifted a new blank surface on which to construct a life that I had only dreamed of.

I didn't know what would happen next. I did know that I now had the faith that if I stayed tuned in, I could have a beautiful future ahead of me that would unfold in the most unexpected of ways.

When I bought hand-sewn masks from a Facebook acquaintance, she asked me to pick them up at her new business—a gorgeous tutoring cottage for homeschool students. It was the hybrid of homeschooling but with the support of teachers that I had been hoping for. Our homeschool journey could continue.

When I mentioned to my friend that Chris had moved out and that I wasn't sure how I would cover my mortgage, she shared that her lease had ended and she and her husband needed a new place to stay. They began renting my downstairs bedroom and also helped me with meal preparation and house and yard maintenance.

By chance, after Chris made it clear that future expansion of our bar business would not include me as an equal owner, my copywriting side hustle suddenly started getting more writing requests. Clients began to find me in the most unusual ways. I stepped away from our "Mom and Pop shop" and launched my copywriting business full time.

As the bank account started to run dry, we refinanced the house at a much lower rate and got an unexpected check back for several thousand dollars.

When Chris and I finally had our divorce hearing, it was held over Zoom on the morning of Oliver's birthday. Chris came over to my house and attended the hearing from his laptop downstairs, while I sat at my laptop upstairs. The judge was kind, and the process was over in approximately two minutes. I came downstairs and we all celebrated Oliver together as a family, though no longer as a legal couple.

And after several members of the Wild-Hearted Collective and I formed a writing group, I started to share my tale of self-discovery. They supported and encouraged me to submit it to Hay House's writing contest. It is this story that you're holding.

I opened my mind to possibility, and the Universe filled in the pieces. My footing was becoming stable. I had made it through the long trek of the messy middle. Now I could stand securely on the shore and enjoy the beauty of the sun rising on an exciting new era ahead.

SAME BUT DIFFERENT

There was one aspect of my life, though, that was still greatly unsettling to me: my relationship with my mom. The distance between us was something I had never expected in my life. I was hurting and so was she, but every time we talked the disconnect became greater. For a while, I just stopped talking. Sticks and stones can break my bones, but words can cause irreparable damage.

I vented to my wildly brilliant and wonderful friend Treisha Peterson. She had just received her Ph.D. in Family Studies and was a huge support to me on my writing journey. Not only did she study identity, perfectionism, and religion, but she was also studying the intricate tie between a mother's identity and the identity of her children. Treisha was also a mom who had lived the experiences that she studied. She was a member of the Church of Jesus Christ of Latter-day Saints and had a gay son. Her virtual support group, the New June Community, centered around women who were navigating identity shifts, motherhood, and belief transitions. If anyone could potentially help me bridge this gap with my mother, it was her.

"Let me draw you a picture," she said over the computer screen as we talked from states away. She drew a dot with circles around it, and then another dot on a different part of the page with circles around it. Some of the circles overlapped. She pointed to the first dot, "This is your coming-out experience. And like a stone you drop in a pond, these circles are the ripples that extend out and affect others." I nodded. I knew the effects of my coming out were felt by those around me. "And this dot over here is your mom. These circles are her own process."

She lost me.

"Your coming-out journey is a different identity experience than what your mom is experiencing," she continued. "You have your own coming out and people feel the effect of that. However, your mom is also undergoing an identity shift now, though different than yours, she will have her own ripples and waves. And although some of your waves are similar, they're not the same."

My large guppy eyes must have looked like a fish out of water trying to understand how my coming out was affecting my mom's life. Shouldn't she just love and accept me?

"Your coming out was a courageous process that you were able to make when you were ready. You likely had done some research, found some allies, and you could decide who you wanted to tell and when. You came out when you felt prepared with the tools to come out." I agreed with her that this was the truth in my coming-out situation. She continued, "For a parent of a gay child, it's different. It can catch them off guard and put them in a situation that they don't have the language to respond to. Our identities as family members are always a little intertwined, and now the LGBTQ+ experience becomes a part of her identity, whether she understands it or not.

The challenge for your mom may be that now she has to process her own feelings around your divorce and coming out, but she can't do that in the same way you do because she may not have a system set up to support her journey.

"When my son came out to me, I couldn't process a lot of my own thoughts and feelings with my husband, because my son was not ready to tell him. I couldn't talk to anyone in my church community, because I did not want to be put in a position where I felt like I had to choose between my faith and my child. I couldn't process with my close friends, because they also knew my son and I didn't want to out him. I had a lot of old beliefs and patterns to unpack, and it can feel really lonely thinking you might have to go through the process alone."

I knew how that felt. Processing alone. Same but different.

"For me, I had to reach far outside of my circle to find people I could process my own thoughts and feelings with as well as find ways to support him without outing him to anyone. They helped, but it was hard for me because I felt like I had restrictions put on how I was able to work through these changes in our lives. I love my son and knew I would fiercely support him, no matter what. But I also knew that the world wouldn't always be kind to him and so I worried for him too. I needed time to consider a lot of what I just didn't know."

It was starting to make more sense, but I felt some frustration bubbling up in me. "So because coming out as the mother of a gay child is hard for my mom, she's allowed to say hurtful stuff to me?! Does she not realize that *she* is the person that is making this the hardest on me? That *her* words have hurt me the most? That all she has to do is love me and trust that I, a grown-ass woman, will be fine?"

Treisha cooled my heated water. "I think your mom really does love you. But she has been flung into a new identity and she doesn't know what to do with it. We don't have language in our society for things like this. We don't know how to have these conversations."

"I just don't understand why she's ashamed of me. There is nothing to be ashamed of. There is nothing wrong with being queer!"

"She's not ashamed of you, but she may need time to process what this means. You may be used to your mom being your solid ground but, for a brief moment, she needs to find her new footing before she can be solid again. It is possible that she is ashamed of the shame she feels. She doesn't want to feel this way. She wants to feel positive and loving and supportive. She feels shame for feeling shame. For me, I wasn't ashamed of my son, but I had a clear understanding of the lessons at church, the messages of our society, and my own fear that I might not be a good enough ally."

"Thank you, Treisha. I think I get it now."

That was the reframing I needed. I had been so focused on how coming out was affecting me, and trying to protect the emotions of Chris and the children, without realizing that we were all on our own journey and timetables. What I had been going through for years, they were just starting in their own different ways. My kids now had a queer mom. Chris would now be the ex-husband of a lesbian. My mom was the parent of a gay child. And as much as we all wanted to be okay with that, we knew that the rest of the world wasn't there yet, and that's where the problem comes in. They were now attached to the stigma of what it means to be LGBTQ+. I didn't choose to be queer, but I did choose to come out. And now they were pulled into that choice.

I sent my mom a text. "We need to talk. There is something I need you to know. Lunch?" She agreed, curious over what it was that I needed her to know that she didn't already know. I consulted my life coach, Jeanna, for some last wise words before entering the conversation. I knew this moment could be another irrevocable shift in my life, for better or worse, based on how I chose my words. I had to make sure my heart was in the right place.

"One of the things I always talk about is our thoughts create how we feel, and thoughts are free for the choosing," Jeanna texted me. "What if you choose the thought, 'I love my mom so much and I love that she's working hard to figure out how she can support me on my journey.'"

I read and reread those words. I had to make sure I did not resort to my usual defensiveness. There was no longer anything that I had to defend. I had to prevent myself from acting like there was.

My mom and I met for poke bowls. We shared awkward hugs, Korean pork buns, and small talk for a bit. And then the conversation shifted.

"What is it you need me to know?" she asked.

There was a stiffening, a wall of protection she was putting up. I understood why. In some of our previous conversations I had fought like a wild grizzly bear to protect myself and my cubs. I realized this defensiveness was no longer needed. My cubs and I were safe and secure in our life. Now I would have to be more like a Care Bear, shooting hearts of compassion from my chest. Perhaps a gentle dose of love could help melt that wall.

I kept it simple. "Mom, I just need you to know that I love you. I just love you and that has never changed." My words had nothing to do with being a lesbian. My words had nothing to do with divorce. There was no work I was asking her to do. Nothing I needed her to change. I had my own ripples in the water. She had her own ripples in the water. And none of that mattered. I just had to let her know that, even with all of the waves, I still loved her.

The wall washed away. We were both in an open space now to have a conversation. We began to pour our hearts out. She asked for specific examples of things she had said that hurt me. I told her directly and honestly. I asked her why she was having such a hard time with my situation. She expressed her concerns for Chris and the kids and her own feelings around divorce and single parenting.

We didn't see eye to eye on things, but finally that was okay with us. It's hard to see eye to eye when you're each standing at different vantage points. We acknowledged that, up until that point, we really didn't have a clear idea of where the other person was standing.

"I'm sorry," she said. "I screwed up. I've said hurtful things that I never meant to be hurtful. My intention was never to be hurtful."

I could feel a healing begin inside of me.

"Teach me," she continued. "Tell me when I'm saying something that hurts your feelings or isn't right. This is all new to me. I don't know what to do." I hugged her. I could finally see and acknowledge her pond ripple and she saw and acknowledged mine. The distance between us had closed slightly.

We celebrated Thanksgiving at my house later that year. Jen joined us. It was not her first time meeting my mom, but it was the first time she, the kids, and I would all be together celebrating a holiday as a family. I planned a few activities to help break the ice. As per usual, our goofy kiddos stepped up to the challenge of entertaining everyone with their antics.

The next morning, I got a text from my mom. "Thanks for a really nice relaxing day. Jen is so sweet. It just feels like she's always been there. Feels like family." My eyes teared up as I passed the phone to Jen. Her eyes did the same.

Dear reader, this chapter is not as easy as it may seem on paper, wrapped up neatly into prose. I am lucky. The relationship with my mom has been rebirthed. We are growing toward each other now, instead of further apart. But it is not a quick process, and we didn't get here because of one conversation with the magical phrases, "I love you" and "I'm sorry." We each had to go through our own growth process to be in a place to even have these conversations.

I began to realize that my previous discussions with my mom were like oobleck, the slime from the Dr. Seuss tale *Bartholomew and the Oobleck*. My kids love making homemade oobleck, a combination of cornstarch and water that, in the right ratio, produces a slime with unusual properties. Oobleck is a non-Newtonian fluid, meaning that when put under stress, its viscosity changes. When Sophie and Oliver try to jam their fingers and hands into the slime, the oobleck responds with resistance, almost like a solid. When they are gentle, resting their fingers on the surface of the oobleck, it melts under their touch and turns to liquid.

With force, it's solid. With gentleness, it softens. I wondered if this is why so many fights between people go nowhere. Perhaps our egos are non-Newtonian fluids as well. My mom and I both had to approach each other gently and without stress in order for the conversation to remain fluid.

Time helped us heal. Time is what helped ease her fears and concerns around the idea that my decision to come out would negatively impact my children, my ex-husband, and my own security. Time proved that those children were still fiercely loved and were provided with a stable environment. Time showed that Chris could find love again and that, while my situation hurt him, he could still stand on his own two feet and move forward. Time demonstrated my resourcefulness in figuring out ways to start my life over and make ends meet while showing up for my children and offering them a better version of myself than I had in the past. With time, we both arrived at a place where there was no longer anything to prove or defend. We could be soft.

Some people will never get to that loving place, even with time. You can still choose to show love to them, if you understand that their problem has nothing to do with you and everything to do with the feelings that your experience has brought up in them. They own those feelings, though, and they are the ones who need to do their own processing. Treisha always lovingly reminded me that there was nothing I could say or do to bring about my mom's own healing. She had to do that work, and that work could never be done with me. If my mom was going to heal, she would need her own resources to do so. I am grateful that we are both doing the work to come together again in a healthier way.

I acknowledge, though, that what happened to me in my coming-out process really is one of the better-case scenarios. Many people who have been through or are going through midlife trauma are not afforded the benefits of a safe home environment, access to therapists, secure friendships, healthy romantic partnerships, and family members and acquaintances willing to work toward understanding. A lack of protection makes recovering from trauma exponentially more difficult.

To those of you in that position, I wish I could reach out and wrap my arms around you in a big hug and remind you that being true to yourself is still one of the greatest gifts you can receive in this lifetime. I would tell you that I am so proud of you for your courage and honesty. I'd rub your back and remind you that living your truth shouldn't have to be this hard and that I'm sorry that it is.

I would whisper to you that where you are now in your life, or relationship, or feelings with someone is not necessarily where you will end up. Things can change. Focus your loving attention on those things within your control. Care for yourself and your boundaries in whatever ways you can. And if you don't feel like you have a community yet, reach out. We are out there to support you. You are not alone in this.

Life doesn't usually go in the direction we plan it to go. People don't usually react the way we want them to react. We can't control the stressors that come our way, but we do have control over how we respond to them. Life is messy. Just like oobleck. I hope that for my children's generation, coming out will be more like Seuss's *Oh, the Places You'll Go!* instead.

THE GAME OF LIFE

I felt like a marathon runner, not seeing a finish line but knowing that I had to be close based on sheer exhaustion and the fact that others' chaffing remarks no longer seemed to hurt so bad. Life was starting to fall into a rhythm, and I realized that this race was not about trying to be better than anyone else; it was about proving to myself that I had a strength I didn't know I was capable of. There was no "perfect" way to do it, just forward motion.

Coming out had a lot of short-term pains. There's shock and grieving, hurtful comments, division of assets, parenting plans, dating woes, and a supersized dose of overall uncertainty. I didn't realize the microhurts I would feel along the way. I remember the first Christmas in separate households, when Chris and I spent the morning together with the kids while they opened their presents. It was their one request when we announced our divorce and we wanted to honor it no matter how difficult it would be for us. I bought Chris a small present, an ornament with a picture of Michael Scott from our favorite show, *The Office*, with the quote "Happy Birthday, Jesus. Sorry Your Party's So Lame." I didn't want to show up empty-handed. He took the package and set it down on the coffee table. It remained unopened. Neither of us knew how to navigate through this. After so many years together, we couldn't imagine not being in each other's lives at all, and yet even friendship felt like a stretch now.

I was always surprised when the microhurts would hit, even after so much time had passed. It hit me on my first Mother's Day with just the kids, and no other parent to make the day special or encourage the kids to create handmade cards. Another single mom reached out that day to see how I was doing. She knew it was going to be tough before I knew it was going to be tough. I was grateful for her simple but thoughtful text messages that day. The microhurts happened during Chris's birthday, when I felt guilt and a responsibility to reach out and do something to make it special, even though I knew that was no longer my place. He had someone special to do that for him. Sometimes microhurts would pop up out of nowhere, when the kids would say something funny or do something amazing, and my first instinct was to want to share the moment with him, but realizing that sharing may just be throwing in his face the fact that he wasn't there for it. The major hurts were over and regular therapy helped me with healing, but the microhurts continued. Tiny tests to see how well Chris and I were both moving on.

I wish I had realized then that all of these major and minor pains, even the ones I still feel today every time my children have to go back and forth between my home and Chris's, can all be short-term issues. With the gift of the passing of time, the beauty of the long-term benefits of living my truth began to shine through. These positives had lifelong staying power.

Coming out as a lesbian changed me as a person in more ways than just having a sudden preference for flannel and Subarus. Sometimes it was in small things, like the fact that I suddenly stopped biting my nails, an annoying habit that I had not been able to kick since my days as a young child. When I started valuing myself and my own needs, my financial life changed as well. I stopped undercharging in my business and started investing. When I finally acknowledged my self-worth, the "money blocks" that financial books had warned me of began to resolve. My house, pool, and yard were now fully my responsibility, and after the fear subsided, I could take care of them. I could learn and do. After overcoming that hill of self-doubt, I realized how many things in my life I put in the "Jill can't do" category that I actually could do. I was adulting at a rapid pace.

A dear college pal of mine, after seeing me post about coming to terms with my sexuality, sent me a private message.

"Can I ask you a personal question?" he started.

"Of course," I replied with curiosity at how personal this was going to get.

"And feel free to tell me to fuck off," he continued. Now I was really intrigued. "Do you feel like you have more of yourself to give your kids now?"

I paused. Nobody had really asked me this before, but I knew the answer immediately.

Coming out profoundly changed the way I parent my children. To be absolutely cliché, you don't realize the weight of something until it's lifted. For me, that weight was the heavy lie I had carried. I loved them and was there for them, but only for as much as I had in me to give. Neither they nor I realized that I was slowly slipping into a depressive fog. But when that fog lifted a few months after Chris moved out and the reality of my new life moved in, I felt like a new parent, and they noticed a new mom.

They now had a whole mom. One who loved herself and could suddenly pour that large amount of love from her cup into theirs. They had a mom who was honest, who felt all the emotions and shared them, and demonstrated how these emotions could be resolved in a healthy way. They had a mom who was intentional with her words and thoughtful in letting them know they were loved for who they were and who they were becoming. I had never felt that mother bear instinct before; this was something that I was ashamed of and chalked up to my early days of postpartum depression. People would say things that would hurt their feelings and I used to brush it off and hope we could deal with it later. Coming out meant pushing people-pleasing to the back burner. I was unapologetically voicing my own needs and now I could protect the needs of my children too.

In coming out, I had gained self-love. With time, I had gained self-worth.

My long-distance relationship with Jen proved to be a benefit in disguise. It allowed my children to slowly acclimate to her, and her to acclimate to our noisy and chaotic days. But when she was with us, it felt like she had always been there. I remember the night Oliver asked me for my phone and called Jen on Facetime. She answered and he immediately hung up. My brain started to prepare a decent-length speech for him on proper phone etiquette and how hanging up on people was rude. But then, from around the corner, I heard him call her back.

"Hi . . . sorry I hung up on you," his little eight-year-old voice squeaked, "I didn't know the words to say." I drew a breath in, waiting.

"That's okay," she responded in her soft voice. "Sometimes I don't know the words to say either." She paused. "We can just look at each other, or we can talk about dogs." That was enough of a start for him that their conversation unfolded with ease and my eyes welled with tears. I love her. And I love them. But seeing how they can also love each other took my heart to a whole new level of fullness.

One time when Jen was with us at our home, we pulled out a board game: *The Game of Life*. It was a new favorite of the kids, except for the first stop sign, Marriage. That stop made the kids groan at the thought of putting a fellow human peg into their car. It felt like an awkward thing for them to have to do at their young age. I snickered at the many comments I had received about my kids being "too young" to learn about same-sex relationships, but having been exposed in numerous ways since birth to heterosexual ones, I had also become aware of the number of signals our society sends to kids about being in a heterosexual relationship and getting married. It's called *compulsory heterosexuality*, or as the cool kids say *comphet*, and is, what I believe, one of the major driving forces in me not coming to terms with my own sexuality for so long. Comphet is simple: it's the message that there is one way to do things. Boys fall for girls; girls fall for boys. You find one you love. You get married. You have babies.

The beautiful thing is that putting an end to comphet in our own children's lives doesn't have to be hard. We can start by using more inclusive language. Instead of peppering youth with "Do you have a boyfriend?" or "Do you have a girlfriend?" you can say, "Are you dating anyone?"

(and even then, if they wanted to tell you they would, so maybe back off, okay?). Conversations on marriage can be more neutral, with terminology like "marrying the person you love" or "choosing a spouse," rather than assuming they'll take a husband or a wife. When it comes to playing Life, I reminded my kids that marriage is not a requirement, nor should it be a goal in life. You get married if that is what you want to do, not because it's what you have to do. Being single is valid. Dating is valid. Choose your own adventure in this life. When we play the game, you can marry a pink peg, you can marry a blue peg, or don't get married and add whomever you want to your car. On Jen's turn, she put a dog in her car. I was offended.

Another beautiful and long-lasting ripple that came from my own public coming out was more people feeling safe to do the same. It was empowering and important to me to come out publicly for myself. I was no longer willing to apologize for my identity. I felt pulled not to hide just for others' comfort. I recognize that a very visible identity is not for everyone, particularly if visibility causes you to feel unsafe.

For me, stepping into my truth felt like that scene in *How the Grinch Stole Christmas!*, when his heart grows three times its size and breaks out of its little wire frame. My spirit grew larger than my physical body. I felt called to put myself out there because it felt like I *was* already out there for people to see. I felt compelled to honor the generations of queer individuals who came before me; both those who stood bravely and took the lead, and those who protected and preserved themselves quietly to survive. And I felt a deep calling to serve the next generations after mine, including that of my children, so that their path ahead might be a bit smoother. My gut told me that

I could be a bridge—for those who loved me when I was straight, I would become their first opportunity to love someone who was queer, perfectly and wonderfully queer. For me, fear of being seen was worth the risk.

Private messages filled my inbox each week as friends, acquaintances, and strangers sought advice or just wanted to share their own stories. Some stories were about being bisexual but in a hetero relationship and feeling unsure if sharing their bisexuality was worth it. One was a woman whose father came out as gay when she was young. He abandoned their family, causing a tremendous amount of hurt. She had a better insight into the shame and pain that may have led him to feel that leaving his family was their best option. One was a woman whose spouse was transitioning to female, and she was struggling to make sense of her relationship and her new perception as a lesbian. I heard from parents of queer kids and teens. Adults who questioned other members of their families. Adults who questioned themselves and just wanted clarity on "the knowing" of queerness.

One that I found particularly touching came from a close friend of mine. She was one of the early people I came out to because she had always felt like a safe space to me, and she was. On the day of my coming out, she poured me a cup of tea and we sat on her barstools talking about life and the unexpected turns it takes. She had been through her own marriage struggles and had lost a husband but gained a tremendous amount of empathy. When our conversation concluded, she gave me a supportive hug and we both went back to regular life where we had to keep it all together as working moms.

A short time later, she decided to share my coming-out story with her teenage daughter and told her daughter how proud she was of me for finally loving and accepting myself and making the hard decision to come out. A few weeks later, her daughter came to her in tears and shared that she thought she might also be queer. She questioned why she had never seemed interested in boys in the way her friends had. Her tears were because she was worried how her mom would react, even after having such a kind and loving reaction to my own coming out. (Sidebar: Coming out is scary—always! Even if someone else has always demonstrated that they are accepting, there is always an underlying fear. Honor that person for their bravery and congratulate yourself for being a safe haven.)

Later my friend shared, "Jill, I sometimes wonder how I would have reacted to my daughter's coming out if you and I hadn't talked first. I knew I would, of course, love her and accept her, but I don't know if I would have known what to say to help her feel secure. I'm so grateful for our talk to prepare me to mother her better and open the door for us to have this conversation. I wonder how long she would have waited to tell me if I had not told her about you." And this is just another reason why I continue to be a vocal representative of the queer community. Our representation in people's lives matters.

The short-term impact of my coming out was hard. The middle is messy, and the pain is heavy. But if you can make it through in a healthy way, with therapy and social support, the long-term effects of coming into your own are so worthwhile, both for you and the people touched by your existence.

We each have the power to give and receive healing. We can each become a truer version of ourselves. Our plants can be repotted so that we grow to be our best. We can gift ourselves permission to bloom.

WORTH IT

I woke up early that cold winter morning. It must have been around 5:55 A.M. because I had just enough time to pull the bedsheets over both of us before I was startled by the sudden sound of the coffee maker grinding beans in the other room at its set 6 A.M. time. I hoped to catch a whiff of its delicious scent in the winter morning's air, but it was too far away and too soon in the process.

So instead I rolled onto my right side next to her. Big spoon position. Feeling the heat coming off her newly reblanketed body and transferring over to me, I decided to slide off my heavy gray sweatpants and opt for just underwear instead. I paused for a moment staring at the outline of her sweet head, her blond hairs brushed backward, the soft shaved spikes of hair on the side of her head around her ears. I took a deep breath in and felt us both exhale at the same time.

I inhaled again. Still no smell of coffee.

With a slight fear of waking her up, and a slight hope that she'd wake up, I pressed myself right up next to her, the front of my knees touching the back of her knees. Her thighs and delicate lace panties resting back into me like I was a chair. I sank my left arm into that beautiful, feminine waist between her ribs and her hips, which became all the more exaggerated in its curve while she was lying on her side. Her curves were poetry in motion to me. I hugged myself to her back and buried my nose into her soft hair, which still smelled like her rosemary mint shampoo.

This is heavenly.

Tears started to fill my eyes in that moment—and now, again, just a few minutes later as I rewrite it, I welled up suddenly with all the emotions that I went through to get here. But no matter how much I could feel the fear, and worry, and anger, and exhaustion, and sadness, and loneliness, and fear . . . did I already say fear? . . . and the fear from the past year and a half, plus a solid lifetime of suppression before that, all I could do was look over at her silhouette against the soft glow of the night-light and feel so overwhelmingly content.

It was all worth it for this moment. All of it.

I debated with myself whether to sneak out of bed and let my thoughts and words pour onto the page, hopefully as quickly as they were coming to my head, or to lay there a bit longer in the moment. I opted to lay there—soaking up the emotion even as the words I wanted to share drifted further from my mind. I hoped the words would come back but also didn't care. This moment was what I had waited and worried and worked for my whole life.

One last deep inhale of gratitude and the scent of the freshly brewed coffee entered my nose, signaling it was time to get up and start writing. I clumsily fumbled out of bed, found my heavy sweatpants, tripped over my overly stuffed computer bag, and played with the hefty sliding barn door of the bedroom in my feeble attempt to not wake her.

I filled my mug. A white one with "This morning with her, having coffee" scrawled on the side. That was Johnny Cash's famous quote of how he defined paradise. I concurred.

As I started to type and grasp for the words that had just been in my mind, the bedroom's barn door slid open and she stood blurry-eyed in the doorway, still in her underwear and old T-shirt.

"There's my beautiful girlfriend. Where did you go?"

She ambled over to the couch where I was sitting and we curled up together, just smiling like goofballs at how cute the other one's puffy morning face was.

"I love you, Jenny," I whispered to her, and I pulled her in for a prolonged hug.

"I love you too," she said back. "I love all the things with you."

I felt another tear come from my eye and roll down my cheek to her shoulder. It was all worth it for this moment. All of it.

EPILOGUE

Fear is what brought me here. While I've looked back on my journey so far, thinking that shame was the overriding emotion, I realized that I was wrong. For me, it has always been fear.

Bronnie Ware's *The Top Five Regrets of the Dying* was published in 2011: four years after I got married and four years after I met Amy. Ware's international best-selling memoir shared the insights and wishes of the terminally ill patients she worked with in their last 12 weeks of life. I figured if I was going to get advice on how to have a good run at this journey, I better learn from those who have done it before they were completely out the door.

The regrets are important and impactful. Sound advice on what they would do if they could do life all over again. I was 30 and figured I probably had at least a few years to put their advice into practice before my own time ran out.

Do you know what was listed as the number one regret? *"I wish I'd had the courage to live a life true to myself, not the life others expected of me."*

That's where fear comes in. The next several years of my life became a balancing act. Those spirits constantly whispered into my ear, reminding me of their regret of not living their truth. It was the regret of living according to societal norms or parental wishes. Was I more afraid of coming out and dismantling my current life or more afraid of being on my deathbed with this secret buried safely within?

You know which fear won out for me in the end.

Thank you for hearing my story. Thank you for taking the time to learn that sexuality has so many layers to it and that "coming out" is more than just opening the closet door. Thank you for understanding that while the LGBTQIA2S+ community has made tremendous progress, there is still so much work to be done in the name of equality and protection. (Or if you're still not convinced, Google "gay panic defense" and see how many U.S. states still allow it as a justification for violence.)

This was my journey from fear and shame to self-love and acceptance. I am grateful that I have had the opportunity to teach these lessons to my children in real time. I want them to know that when people say, "It's what's on the inside that counts," that it is the truth.

And now, I leave you with this final thought. Your story might be complicated. Your story might be confusing. Your story may have had more than its fair share of challenges. But you are the author of your own life story. And it's not too late to write a new ending.

ENDNOTES

1. LePera, Nicole. *How to Do the Work: Recognize Your Patterns, Heal from Your Past, and Create Your Self*, (London: Orion Spring, 2021), 75.

2. Ibid, 40.

3. Ibid, 146.

4. Grace Medley et al., "Sexual Orientation and Estimates of Adult Substance Use and Mental Health: Results from the 2015 National Survey on Drug Use and Health," National Survey on Drug Use and Health (Oct. 2016). https://www.samhsa.gov/data/sites/default/files/NSDUH-SexualOrientation-2015/NSDUH-SexualOrientation-2015/NSDUH-SexualOrientation-2015.htm.

5. American Psychological Association, APA RESOLUTION on Sexual Orientation, Gender Identity (SOGI), Parents and their Children (Feb. 2020): 4. https://www.apa.org/about/policy/resolution-sexual-orientation-parents-children.pdf.

ABOUT THE AUTHOR

Jillian Abby has always wanted to be a writer. But she thought it wasn't what she was supposed to do—that somehow that dream was just reserved for the likes of Dr. Seuss, Stephen King, and E. L. James. If there is one thing she has learned on this journey, though, it's that when our intuition speaks, it's best to listen. Since then, Jillian has become an expert in course-correcting when life does not feel aligned with its purpose.

Jillian now writes from her heart through her copywriting firm, Jill iNK, and on her blog site QueerAbby.com. She is committed to using her voice to uplift the stories of others and create a more equitable world for the LGBTQIA2S community through her podcast, *Life and Love in the Q*. She's a member of the Tampa Bay LGBT Chamber of Commerce and serves on the board of Tampa Bay Homeschool Inclusive Events, Inc.

Jillian lives in Tampa Bay with her two wildly wacky children; her soul human, Jen; and their rescue cat, Poe. She strives to spend as much time as possible in a hammock with an iced coffee in hand.